CONTEMPORARY STAGE DESIGN
U.S.A.

CONTEMPORARY STAGE DESIGN
U.S.A.

Edited by
Elizabeth B. Burdick, Peggy C. Hansen and Brenda Zanger

INTERNATIONAL THEATRE INSTITUTE OF THE UNITED STATES, INC.
Distributed by Wesleyan University Press, Middletown, Connecticut

Library of Congress Catalog Card Number: 74-26233
Designed and produced by Jack Doenias
Type set by Film Comp, Inc., New York
Printed by Eastern Press, Inc., New Haven
Bound by Sendor Bindery, Inc., New York

This book enables the International Theatre Institute
not only to celebrate stage design in the United States,
but also to offer visible thanks to those who have supported the exhibition
Contemporary Stage Design–U.S.A., this book, and the work of ITI.
Our sincere appreciation is extended to
The Peter C. Cornell Trust
The Ford Foundation
The JDR 3rd Fund
The Andrew W. Mellon Foundation
National Endowment for the Arts
New York State Council on the Arts
Rockefeller Brothers Fund
The Shubert Foundation, Inc.

INTERNATIONAL THEATRE INSTITUTE OF THE UNITED STATES, INC.

The International Theatre Institute was chartered by UNESCO in 1948 "to promote the exchange of knowledge and practice in the theatre arts." Eleven nations were represented at the charter meeting in Prague, Czechoslovakia. Today, ITI centers exist in 60 countries around the world, with a central office at UNESCO headquarters in Paris.

The International Theatre Institute of the United States, Inc. (ITI/US) is an independent, non-profit, service organization.

ITI/US exists to serve the needs of theatre professionals and to further communication among theatre people around the world. In practice, these aims are reflected in special projects, such as the Contemporary Stage Design—U.S.A. exhibit and book, and in continuing programs: foreign visitor services, publications, information exchange, library and research, representation at theatre meetings.

ITI/US STAFF: Rosamond Gilder *President,* Martha W. Coigney *Director,* Maurice McClelland *Associate Director,* Peggy C. Hansen *Assistant Director,* Elizabeth B. Burdick *Library Director,* Crawford K. Wright *Library Assistant,* Brenda Zanger *Exhibition Coordinator,* Esther Williams *Secretary*

BOARD OF DIRECTORS: Martha W. Coigney, Eldon Elder, Rosamond Gilder, David E. LeVine, Porter McCray, Harold Prince, Ellen Stewart, George C. White

CONTEMPORARY STAGE DESIGN—U.S.A. STEERING COMMITTEE: Ming Cho Lee *Chairman,* Howard Bay, Martha W. Coigney, Eldon Elder, Rosamond Gilder, Donald Oenslager, Joel Rubin, Brenda Zanger

CONTEMPORARY STAGE DESIGN—U.S.A. ADVISORY PANEL: Boris Aronson, Clive Barnes, Patton Campbell, John Canaday, Gordon Davidson, Charles Elson, Zelda Fichandler, Emily Genauer, Jane Greenwood, Henry Hewes, Robert Joffrey, Porter McCray, Jo Mielziner, Tharon Musser, Alwin Nikolais, Robert O'Hearn, Joseph Papp, Jerome Robbins, Alan Schneider, Michael Schultz, Hans Sondheimer, Roger L. Stevens, Patricia Zipprodt

CONTEMPORARY STAGE DESIGN—U.S.A. SELECTION COMMITTEE: Howard Bay, Patton Campbell, Eldon Elder, Emily Genauer, Robert Joffrey, Ming Cho Lee, Albert Marre, Donald Oenslager, Alan Schneider, Patricia Zipprodt

CONTENTS

CONTEMPORARY STAGE DESIGN
U.S.A.

Shock has its uses. It calls attention; it demands action; it can be creative, as in the case of the exhibition Contemporary Stage Design—U.S.A. Two shocks and a surprise went into launching the design exhibit of which this book is a record. The first shock came when the world-wide scene design exhibition known as the Quadrennial opened in Prague in 1967 without any United States representation. The second shock occurred four years later when the second Prague Quadrennial still showed no U.S. work, not, it should be noted, for lack of official invitation. But that year, 1971, with the International Organization of Scenographs and Theatre Technicians holding its Congress at the same time and in the same place, a number of American scene designers were present and their dismay triggered this exhibition.

The surprise element stemmed from another source. The Steering Committee[1] set up to organize the project discovered to its astonishment that there has never been a nationwide stage design exhibit in the United States. There have been numberless individual and group shows, some including the work of foreign artists, but never a stage design exhibit drawing solely upon the work of designers from the far-flung American theatre—the resident, regional, university and professional theatres from New York to Honolulu and back. Contemporary Stage Design—U.S.A. is the first.

When the shocked designers returned to New York from Prague, they came to the International Theatre Institute of the United States with the demand that something be done about the absence of American artists from the international exhibition scene. The ITI/US shared the shock and accepted the challenge on condition that the scenic artists themselves take the lead in planning, judging and launching the project. At first geared only for participation in the third Prague Quadrennial (1975), the project came to serve a necessary, larger and further purpose. It was time that the remarkable achievements of American scenic artists be better known in the United States itself and that a stage design exhibit of national importance be mounted.

As shock gave way to planning, three major problems had to be solved: how to reach the artists, young and old, near and far, who might wish to take part in the event; how to select a reasonable number of designs and models which would reflect the variety and richness of the American scene; and finally, how to cover the costs of such a national and international endeavor. The first step was to announce the project to all the regional and university theatres and to all members of the United Scenic Artists and other specialized groups, since the Committee envisaged showing design for every type of theatre presentation, from the Broadway musical through opera, dance and experimental productions of all kinds.

A major obstacle to developing the full potential of Contemporary Stage Design—U.S.A. as a comprehensive exhibition was the method of work of the American designer in recent years. Once academic training is completed, the designer rarely has the time to paint pretty pictures of his designs or complete a handsome model. More often rough models suffice to show the director the spatial arrangements, while small, rough sketches are used to illustrate the stylistic concept.

The difficulty for the scenic artist is manifest. Scene design and lighting are inseparable, and no sketch, model, photograph or rendering can ever give the full impact of such work. Further, as Robert Edmond Jones once said, "The essence of the stage setting lies in its incompleteness . . . . It is charged with a sense of expectancy. It awaits the actor and not until the actor has made his entrance does it become an organic whole."

Fully aware of these problems, the design members of the Steering Committee devoted many long hours to selecting from some 2,000 photographs and slides sent in from all over the country those designs to be viewed in their original forms. In judging the designs, the Committee knew only the subject of the rendering or model which they were viewing, not the name or the experience of the artist. The designer might be a graduate student or a veteran of 25 years on Broadway.

In September 1974, an expanded Selection Committee[2] viewed the original works. The 250 designs, renderings and models, which make up the exhibition are the result of the careful and conscientious work of that group of truly generous professionals whose names should be written in gold at the head of this brief introduction to Contemporary Stage Design—U.S.A. Nor should those who have provided the absolutely necessary funds for collecting, framing, transporting and caring for this unique exhibit have any less honor and appreciation.[3] Looking at the "pictures on the wall" and the pages of this book in which the exhibition is permanently recorded, we believe that the shock experienced by some of us at the first and second Prague Quadrennials has had most splendid results.

Contemporary Stage Design—U.S.A. makes its bow at the Library and Museum of the Performing Arts at Lincoln Center, a highly appropriate locality since stage design for theatres, operas, ballets and street scenes is probably in greater demand here than in any other comparable spot in the world. Following its three-month stay at Lincoln Center, the exhibition will appear at the Kennedy Center in Washington, D.C., travel to Prague for the third Quadrennial, stop over in London if the new National Theatre is completed, return for a tour of New York State and finally, and importantly, tour the United States for two years under the aegis of SITES (Smithsonian Institution Traveling Exhibition Service). The SITES tour will bring the exhibit into the U.S. Bicentennial celebrations on a nationwide scale.

It would appear that Contemporary Stage Design—U.S.A. is in for a long run.

Rosamond Gilder
New York City, 1974

1. Howard Bay, Martha W. Coigney, Eldon Elder, Rosamond Gilder, Ming Cho Lee (Chairman), Donald Oenslager, Joel Rubin, Brenda Zanger (Project Coordinator).
2. Howard Bay, Patton Campbell, Eldon Elder, Emily Genauer, Robert Joffrey, Ming Cho Lee, Albert Marre, Donald Oenslager, Alan Schneider, Patricia Zipprodt.
3. See Acknowledgments, page 5.

U.S. STAGE DESIGN—PAST AND PRESENT

Donald Oenslager

Today, stage design is recognized throughout the United States as an established profession, whether on Broadway or Off Broadway, or in the regional or educational theatre. Wherever he works, the designer is an artist and craftsman who translates the world around him into the theatrical terms of the stage.

Yet it was only 60 years ago that the "stage designer" as we know him today began to play a part in the American theatre. His 19th-century counterpart was the resident scenic artist, who was one of the family group of every theatre. E.T. Harvey was resident scenic artist in Pike's Opera House in Cincinnati; Thomas Glessing (intimate friend of Joseph Jefferson) presided over the paint frame high above the stage of English's Theatre in Indianapolis and later the Boston Athenaeum. In New York, Charles Witham was the chief scenic artist of Booth's Theatre and later Daly's.

To meet the increasing demand for scenery, scenic studios (staffed with specialized scenic artists) were established in large cities: Sosman and Landis in Chicago, and in New York Lee Lash, Unitt and Wickes, Gates and Morange. Those scenic "factories" turned out readily designed, realistic scenic productions for the theatre manager. Most of these emporiums also conducted a large mail-order business, providing scenery for hundreds of theatres all over the country.

By the turn of the century, producer-director David Belasco had become the self-appointed monarch of realism. For his setting of a Parisian garret, he dispatched his agent to France to seek out and strip the wallpaper and furnishings from an old attic and installed them on his stage. In lighting *The Girl of the Golden West,* he achieved the golden verisimilitude of a sunrise over the California Sierras. His wizardry led the theatre into a hopeless dead end of false realism.

Many forces diverted the visual course of the American theatre from the scenic doldrums of those years before World War I. Gordon Craig and Adolphe Appia, self-proclaimed prophets of the New Movement in the theatre, were assaulting all the false façades of realism. In New York their lofty concepts and inspired designs for the modern theatre influenced three young designers, Robert Edmond Jones, Lee Simonson and Norman Bel Geddes. Each was dedicated to implanting on Broadway his revolutionary vision of the new stagecraft. With their bold experimentation, this coura-

above Norman Bel Geddes: model for Dante's *Divine Comedy,* 1921
Scene: Paradise, "O! Thou sweet light..."
below Robert Edmond Jones: *Macbeth,* 1921

geous triumvirate brought visual style and dramatic excitement to the American theatre for 30 years. Early in those years, Joseph Urban was summoned from Vienna to the Boston Opera House and then to the Metropolitan Opera in New York to set new scenic standards for the production of opera. With Florenz Ziegfeld, he brought stunning vitality to the musical stage. In 1923, these artists, with their fellow designers, Aline Bernstein, Claude Bragdon, Raymond Sovey and Woodman Thompson, affiliated themselves with Local 829 of United Scenic Artists and established the tradition and the profession of stage design in the New York theatre.

Lee Simonson: *Dynamo,* 1929

At that same time, a unity of artistic direction appeared spontaneously among aspiring Off Broadway groups—the Washington Square Players (forerunner of the Theatre Guild), the Neighborhood Playhouse, the New Playwrights, and the Provincetown Players–Greenwich Village Theatre. These experimental theatres were the early proving ground for many talented playwrights, actors, directors and designers. Many were dreaming of revolutionary forms of new theatre architecture. Joseph Urban and titanic Norman Bel Geddes were tearing away not only the old scaffolding that concealed the new theatre, but even the proscenium arch itself. Stimulus to the New Movement was also provided by many designers among insurgent civic art theatres mushrooming throughout the country. The expanding educational theatre contributed its share of explosive talent to this ever-broadening flood stream of the modern American theatre.

Our burgeoning theatre received visits from sundry troupes of the Great World Theatre—Diaghilev, Mei Lan-Fang, Stanislavski and Max Reinhardt were but a few. Each submerged us in a tidal wave of stylistic wonder. Each administered its own peculiar antidote for the old realism. Our theatre responded to the treatment—whether it was Symbolism, Expressionism or Constructivism. Many productions of the 1920's glowed with pictorial overtones of Freud, machine worship and futuristic art.

Already a younger group of aspiring designers—among them Boris Aronson, Mordecai Gorelik, Jo Mielziner and Donald Oenslager—were serving their apprenticeship in experimental theatres or assisting the founding designers. During Broadway's boom years of the late 1920's, they were designing their first productions with already established directors like Guthrie McClintic, George Abbott, George S. Kaufman, Philip Moeller, John Houseman, Jed Harris and Harold Clurman. There were stimulating plays to design by foreign authors and by our own playwrights—Maxwell Anderson, Philip Barry, Sidney Howard, Sidney Kingsley, Eugene O'Neill and Robert E. Sherwood.

What were the visual trends of that dynamic theatre? The swift-paced techniques of motion pictures and television influenced multi-scene methods of theatrical production. Before long, younger playwrights, Tennessee Williams and Edward Albee, would welcome from designers innovative scenic ideas which imaginatively suggested locale and mood. Such a setting, composed of a skeletal arrangement of semi-transparent scenes, contributed a fourth-dimensional quality to the stage picture. Light pursued the action of the play from one scene to another and provided the audience with an x-ray image of the entire stage picture. Playwrights like Thornton Wilder and Arthur Miller relied on the designer to help formulate their minimal scenic needs. Some plays required almost no scenery—only the stage's bare walls enclosing a wide-open, atmospheric-space stage. In designing these plays, mobile lighting became the designer's primary medium of expression, a motivating force which illuminated and supported the dramatic action of the playwright.

During the 1930's and 1940's, most of the New York designers, including new arrivals on the scene (among them, Ralph Alswang, Lemuel Ayers, Howard Bay, Stewart Chaney, Charles Elson, Frederick Fox, Harry Horner, Albert Johnson and Sam Leve), applied their skills and talents, some to bringing theatrical style to opera, others to the development of the Broadway musical theatre of George Gershwin, Jerome Kern, Cole Porter, Richard Rodgers and Arthur Schwartz. In this jamboree, authors, composers, choreographers, directors and designers combined to exercise their fancy-free talents in transforming the American musical into a unique flowering of American theatrical art.

Also in the 1940's, Agnes de Mille, Martha Graham, and the versatile choreographers of the New York City Ballet and the American Ballet Theatre discovered visual stimulus for their costumes and scenes in the fresh talents of Oliver Smith, Rouben Ter-Arutunian and painters and sculptors like Eugene Berman, Pavel Tchelitchew and Isamu Noguchi.

Significantly, at that time, a group of trained lighting designers entered the theatre. They were aware of the importance of theatrical lighting and were sensitive in collaborating with those designers, directors and choreographers who had no technical knowledge of stage lighting. Three enlightened women who had studied with Stanley McCandless in the Yale Drama School, Jean Rosenthal, Tharon Musser and Peggy Clark, were the pioneers in this field, along with Abe Feder. They were followed by Martin Aronstein, Jules Fisher, John Gleason and others. With their expertise, all have made significant contributions to the art of the theatre.

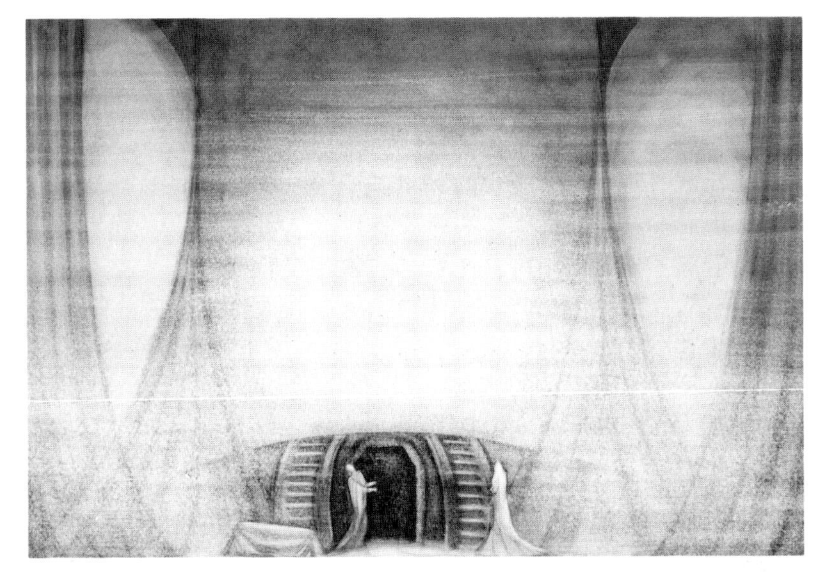

above Donald Oenslager: *Tristan und Isolde,* 1934
Scene: *"Isolde's Ship"*
below Jo Mielziner: *Winterset,* 1935

Lemuel Ayers: *Oklahoma!*, 1943

Following the downbeat of World War II, the fractured Broadway invalid was soon out of traction. But beneath the placid surface of the advancing theatre were felt increasing rumblings of recession from all sides. In the 1950's, a group of intern designers were already assessing the state of the theatre and applying their therapy to the Broadway scene. Robert O'Hearn, Will Steven Armstrong, William and Jean Eckart, Ben Edwards, Eldon Elder, George Jenkins, Peter Larkin and others succeeded brilliantly in applying their aesthetics of stage design to inventing styles of scenic simplification to conform with the increasingly limited budgets of Broadway managers.

Happily our theatre is never at ease. For three quarters of a century, the art of stage design has been a continuously changing art. This does not necessarily imply that there is a revolutionary moment when one style of design is categorically rejected and another assumed. For example, the battle of the proscenium theatre and the non-proscenium theatre is not suddenly lost or won. The designer functions equally well in both. Witness the next decade of avant-garde designers, each with his will to do the theatre over in his own image—among them, David Hays, Ming Cho Lee, William Ritman, Fred Voelpel and Ed Wittstein. They found their release in experimenting in untried scenic conventions and new theatre forms not only on Broadway, but significantly Off Broadway and in the new regional theatres and opera houses across the U.S. Everywhere, designers discovered that the American theatre was on the move, changing its course, assuming community responsibilities and discovering new relationships between audience and performers.

Those designers' successors are today's youngest designers with their proud manifestoes for tomorrow's theatre. Among them are Edward Burbridge, John Conklin, Eugene Lee, Santo Loquasto, Jerry Rojo, Douglas Schmidt, Robert U. Taylor and Peter Wexler. They seek out fresh identity. Many are peripatetic designers preferring to move from theatre to theatre cross-country, like the journeymen scenic artists before them. Theirs is a theatre that has survived the theatre. Their liberated settings combine realistic, abstract, multi-media and environmental scenic techniques. They are at home on proscenium, thrust, arena and open stages. There is confidence in the vigor and strength of this newest generation.

Stage design of the past decade in America mirrors the unrest and turbulence of the changing American scene. Three generations of designers working in the professional, regional and educational theatre have participated in transforming our American theatre into the wide-ranging, tumultuous, utterly disorganized institution it is today. No cohesive Modern Movement galvanizes the American theatre of today as it did the New York theatre of the 1920's and 1930's. Walter Kerr has observed that "our theatre is struggling to give birth to itself all over again on a dozen different fronts." Today's designers are searching for new boundaries to contain the theatre of the last quarter of the 20th century. This is apparent in the vitality and variety of the designs in this exhibition, which reflects the conscience of the contemporary American theatre.

THE DESIGNER AND THE BROADWAY SCENE

Howard Bay

above Stewart Chaney: *Parnell,* 1935
below Jo Mielziner: *Pal Joey,* 1940

It is fruitless to string together all-but-forgotten names of Broadway's fugitive attractions and the designers who furnished the pictorial embellishments. Perhaps we can pin down the atmosphere of the creation of commercial scenic art by recalling snippets from My Life on the Great White Way.

I led a sheltered childhood nourished by the rhapsodic prose and exhilarating projects of Edward Gordon Craig. Marooned on the Great Plains, I was saved from exposure at a tender age to the Brothers Shubert and the pillars of the Theatre Guild—or today I would be in some other line of endeavor. With an impeccable sense of timing, I descended on New York with portfolio in the very depths of the Depression. It wasn't exactly Magic Time. The artistic settings by the name designers reproduced in *Theatre Arts Monthly* were few and far between. The standard produce filling up the prosceniums were large boxes with several doors, most everything painted apple green, or oatmeal with gold for high-toned locales.

I failed to find employment drafting up the rectangles for the scenic factories, but the national government stepped in. The Federal Theatre was a fine laboratory for the designer-in-the-making. In contrast to the automatic, departmentalized mode of manufacturing commercial entertainment, the W.P.A. team of producer, director and designer enthusiastically kicked around a production concept until it jelled into a unique piece of theatre. The very format of Living Newspaper inspired innovation. We spotted and tagged scraps of tenements that were scheduled for demolition: balustrades, rusty stamped-tin ceilings, crumbling cornices (after delousing) became part of a stage structure, along with breakaway burlesque props and the hand-tinted Biblical slides of a barnstorming revivalist. A stage-struck gent, who happened to own a scaffolding firm, delivered a pipe construction that would hold up a small building in the outside world. All this ferment had to spill over into the marketplace and loosen up the staid set dressing. It gave me the gall to march into a regular scenic shop with a slab of moldy Swiss cheese and declare that I wished the entire setting to be painted "just like this specimen here." However, economics dictated that those three-sided-boxes-with-tops were our steady fare.

As actors are typecast, so are designers. For the longest time I seemed to be engaged on nothing but hyper-realistic depressed areas and Victorian gingerbread. I envied Donald Oenslager and

Stewart Chaney for their posh drawing rooms with Ilka Chase ensconced on the satin divans. I had a spot of trouble once with my rickety gingerbread. I invented a ramshackle Arizona boarding-house which displeased the producer, a gentleman hitherto concerned with Grade C westerns. Everyone knows that the Southwest has only adobe Spanish haciendas with Navajo rugs thrown over the balconies, and what did I mean tinkering with nature? Generally, producers of plays were one generation behind audiences; their incestuous world seldom extended beyond Lindy's and the Lambs Club. It is difficult to recapture that period in the annals of the stage wherein we worried ourselves sick over the right combination of stock moldings on a cornice at the top of a set. Technical polish and slick mechanics we turned out in our sleep—such as it was.

Tired of antimacassars and ash trays and deep motivations, I glanced wistfully across Shubert Alley at my brethren of musical comedy who appeared to be having more fun. This was during the stretch when the decor for a musical was not considered the genuine article if it didn't look like a Raoul Dufy. My baptism with music was a presentation in which the big production number was titled "The Woman Behind the Man Behind the Gun" . . . then came Mike Todd. The only point in dragging in Todd at this late date is that he personified an attitude that has been lost and had better be recaptured if theatre is to hold a sizable audience. This was the showman's catering to the need for spectacle, for excitement, and for colorful splash in the scenic production. For all the excruciating corn and dumb numbers, musicals really were more exhilarating for a simple reason: the American musical theatre is an exuberant collaboration of musicians, writers, producers, directors, choreographers and designers—we create on the wing.

Dealing with the straight drama is too often a passive, interpretive chore, bogged down in frayed trivia that doesn't excite the audience. The musicals went their merry way, frowned on by the serious arm of Broadway, until that day arrived when the serious folks found themselves borrowing from the musicals. This came to pass when dramatists started breaking up the solid act blocks and stringing together tenuous strands of episodes. Obviously, the full stage picture had to go. To begin with, the musicals always sported a portal framing and never pretended the customers were gazing into the firmament (even an improved firmament with the union label in the corner). The musicals always shuttled scenic fragments around on wheels—tabloid indications of locale. The straight designers borrowed the cutouts, the gauzes, the open stages, the machinery; and before long, the fragmented set pieces were pared down to wire tracery.

Oliver Smith: *Brigadoon,* 1947

The toothpick skeletons are still with us as our prime cliché. I somehow never pictured Winesburg, Ohio, as a jungle gym. *The Desperate Hours* just wouldn't work with spidery calligraphy instead of my solid carpentry, while *The Glass Menagerie* was properly set with Jo Mielziner's delicate framing and ambiguous, moody gauzes. The period-book musical resurrected the flappy painted canvas (*Oklahoma!, Bloomer Girl, Up in Central Park, High Button Shoes, The Music Man*) and slowed down the antiseptic outline craze. These shows, in which the detailed nostalgia conjured up a fairy-book Americana, were the last stand of pictorial scenic art.

Howard Bay: *Up in Central Park,* 1945

These same productions also illustrate an essential step in the design process, namely, research. By the time that *Up in Central Park* was unveiled to the paying customers, I could have reconstructed the park to Olmsted and Vaux's satisfaction. Scrounging through the dusty archives at the Building Department, unearthing views and descriptions of the work in progress, getting sidetracked by the juicy shenanigans of Boss Tweed and his political pals: it all piled up, sorted out, was refined and ultimately provided the right, inevitable flavor to the physical production. Erudition per se is not the designer's aim in life, but the data of how people lived in historical epochs and in far-flung places is the requisite raw material for creating appropriate living space for stage characters.

While we are on the subject, we might quickly run through the procedure of designing for Broadway. The designer seldom has a signed contract until late in the day because the monies are tardy in getting to the bank. For a guide, we have a "rough" script that may be switched from 17th-century London to present-day Bloomingdale's—hinging on whether the star can be crammed into pants. The producer, who made his packet in soft goods, or rather his father did, bumped into this divine frail at Maxwell's Plum last night who definitely said that it all must look Art Deco, definitely. The director, who was the producer's roomie at Yale, fresh from his triumph of staging the bare-assed *Perils of Mary Magdalene* Off Off Broadway, is seized with the gut reaction that only mixed media is viable today. The writer, whose credits peak to a documentary on foreplay in the elementary schools, is mandated by his Dramatists Guild contract to have a voice in everything.

Now, our designer, poised in front of clean tracing paper on his drawing board, embarks on the job of dreaming up concrete scenery that will be delivered in New Haven three and a half weeks hence. He his buttressed by the array of research mentioned above. Like designers everywhere, he doodles with fanciful thoughts until a concept takes shape so real scenery can be drafted to scale. What differentiates the Broadway artist-craftsman from others of the species is the breakneck speed of the operation; the balancing of the widely disparate backstages that have been booked; the iron necessity of holding the operational crews to the minimum by devising clever mechanisms; the hectic and simultaneous production of renderings, working drawings, scenic elevations, prop drawings, light plots; the search for drapery and upholstery fabrics, furniture, dressing, foliage, carpeting; plus the daily visits to the widely separated shops that are turning out the artwork.

What compounds this frenzy is the one-show economy of Broadway. Script, monies, cast and staff are patched together for each venture and are dispersed at its completion. This slaphappy routine is extra hard on the designers for two reasons. First, the squeezed calendar hits the ones who must order solid things in advance, such as scenery and costumes. To alter the words requires only an eraser. Second and more important, the absence of continuity in staff, crews and execution firms leads to a skimpiness of communication in the telescoped time available to put together a show.

The meager stipend doled out to Broadway designers has a silver lining (well, a sequin lining): having to perpetually labor for bread, the designers cover a wide variety of productions and problems and thereby become *the* backstage experts. Producers wander in from respectable commerce, directors and writers vacation from TV; but the designing fraternity deals daily and nightly with counterweights, winches, switchboards, blacksmiths, castors, fabric houses, squawk boxes, hardware, antique peddlers, stars, fitting rooms, budgets, breakaway mountains, Teflon, fog gadgets, celastic armor, and relief help from the corner bar.

It might not be amiss to speculate on present and future trends in designing for the commercial stage. The psychedelic 1960's left only superficial scars—a few sheets of Mylar and some flashing strobes. The ad-lib handling of projections Off Broadway didn't transplant to Broadway, although there were some financially painful tries. The worthwhile work in projections is still limited to the opera houses and permanent companies of Central Europe. The valiant effort to demolish the proscenium arch has calmed down to an expansion of aprons over orchestra pits. What has taken hold, particularly in mountings of Shakespeare, is the use of hefty carved blocks unearthed from archaic sites. This stylistic tendency which is a search for stable, majestic roots is technically possible with today's styrofoam, vacuum casting and sprayed plastics.

Overall, there is a more sophisticated treatment of stage space with the death of the full-stage pictures revealed by the raising of a velvet curtain. Today, changing scenery in view of the audience is an accepted convention. Variations of assemblage and collage have finally made it through the stage door. In the prophecy line, I believe we will drift towards an airy collage of elements that appear and disappear, visually complementing the flow of the drama. "Drift" is the key word—as we do not theorize much around Sardi's. However, we had better have emblazoned over our drawing boards some inspirational saying that reminds us that color and excitement are unique to the living theatre and that the designer is responsible for a healthy portion of such glamour.

By definition, a stage designer is an underpaid masochist. Yes, but on the rare evening in midtown Manhattan when the glistening lights come up on a buoyant, carefree musical wherein everything is meshed to perfection—story, music, lyrics, performers, sets, costumes—the designer feels he is part of something that is special to the U.S.A. and the crummy Broadway marketplace. He might even dissipate and order champagne.

ENVIRONMENTAL DESIGN

Jerry N. Rojo

Jerry N. Rojo: rendering for *Makbeth,* 1970

The term environmental theatre defines an aesthetic approach to production. It provides highly controlled conditions so that transactions involving performer, space and text may be developed organically. The antecedents of environmental theatre can be found in the theories and practices of Meyerhold and Artaud, and more recently in the work of Grotowski, Gregory and Schechner. Major influences derive from guerrilla theatre, street theatre, happenings, and from the work of the Absurdists. In the last few years, the exploration of improvisational acting techniques, performer game theory, psychophysical actor theory, and ensemble workshop dynamics has generated new approaches evident in environmental production. Within the structure of games and improvisations, the performing ensemble discovers and defines dramatic actions that are based on immediate social, physical and spatial conditions.

Probably the single most important environmental theatre concept, so far as the designer is concerned, is the idea of *mise en scène*, or living action in time and space. The environmentalist begins with the notion that the production will both develop from and totally inhabit a given space; and that, for the performer and audience, time, space and materials exist as what they are and only for their intrinsic value. All aesthetic problems are solved in terms of actual time, space and materials with little consideration given to solutions that suggest illusion, pretense or imitation. An environment, for example, never creates an illusion of, say, a forest, although actors and audience may discover danger literally in a precarious arrangement of platforms, or a sense of safety may be achieved where a high place is conquered. In the more traditional theatre experience, the production is appreciated from *outside*, in a world especially created for the relatively passive observer. In the environmental experience, on the other hand, appreciation generates from *within* by virtue of shared activity. Each environmental production creates a sense of total involvement.

The scope of the environmental designer's responsibility extends to organizing the total space, selecting materials, determining construction technique, and considering the associational and intrinsic value of each aspect of design. The traditional division of space into lobby, stage, technical areas, backstage and auditorium is, in this kind of theatre, no longer considered to be immutable, but is subject to organization and reorganization according to a particular production concept. Traditionally, spatial arrangements are imposed on a production, as in theatres with fixed seating. The environmentalist, however, feels that aesthetic considerations should determine movement and actor-audience arrangements.

Typically the environmental designer's impulse begins with architectural and engineering considerations because he has to serve a new kind of physically oriented actor, an actively participating audience and a concept that views space, time and action in terms of an immediate living experience. Therefore, the designer is concerned with the total disposition of space and its related problems—not only problems of production, but also those involved with building codes, safety, comfort, public services, and the peculiar engineering and construction difficulties that arise when a whole complex of theatre experiences is placed under one roof. Thus, in the environmental production, the interaction and negotiation between performers and audience require a sharing of facilities which implies not so much stage design but architecture. In essence, the designer becomes a hybrid architect-designer who conceives of a totally new theatre for each production.

These architecture-oriented designs began to proliferate in the late 1960's with the work of Eugene Lee and with my own work. Such designs as my *Makbeth,* in 1969, and Lee's *Slave Ship,* 1970, are early examples. The production of *Makbeth,* done by Richard Schechner's Performance Group, utilized an ambitious environmental design that was architectural in scope. There had been earlier environmental theatre experiments, but this production confronted and engaged the audience and performer in a new kind of spatial dynamics. In the Performing Garage a massive structure was built—which, incidentally, attracted the unfavorable attention of city building officials. This radical structure presented complex problems involving public occupancy and theatre building codes; and negotiations between architect, designer, fire marshal and building inspector failed to result in certification for the theatre. The production finally opened with temporary approval while negotiations proceeded.

Makbeth was unique because, for the first time, for all practical purposes, a theatre was built to achieve a specific production idea. The production took place in a four-story environment which had a base 50 by 35 feet and a total height of 34 feet. The experience began in Brooks McNamara's upstairs environment which combined ticket-buying with contemporary images related to the play.

Jerry N. Rojo: *Makbeth,* 1970

above Jerry N. Rojo: *Endgame,* 1973
below Jerry N. Rojo: *The Tooth of Crime,* 1973

This part of the production was, for the audience, a non-performer activity which took place while the performers were engaged in preparatory work in the main environment below. Entrance into the main environment, which I designed, was accomplished by descending from the maze by a spiral staircase. The spectator was offered a panorama that forced an immediate and intense confrontation with traditional views about auditorium and stage. Scenery, auditorium, stage, aisles and seats became in *Makbeth* an environmental conglomerate to which all participants had certain rights according to the production concept. In the purest sense, anyone who came into the space, whether performer, spectator, technician or attendant, had "a piece of the action." The staircase, ramps, ladders and platforms were actively used by all the participants all the time; performers and audience alike were forced by the nature of the environment to engage each other's territory. All groups negotiated with the environment on their own terms. There was little concern for illusion, mood or spectacle in the usual sense; instead the artist's energy was applied to solving architectural problems that derived from the concept of a functional living theatre.

Eugene Lee is another designer who represents the environmental approach to design. In 1970, for the Chelsea Theatre Center, he designed *Slave Ship,* which was a production that involved audience and performer in an entire theatre space experience. As in subsequent designs, he stripped the inside of a traditional proscenium theatre in order to freely meet the spatial demands of production. The entire theatre became a slave ship. In keeping with environmental theatre precepts, the space relationships augmented the content of the play in that a center bi-leveled platform suggested the "main deck" with the "slave quarters" below. The audience internally shared the event as the performers played among them from stations which alluded to the spatial structure of a ship.

The Manhattan Project's production of *Endgame,* directed by Andre Gregory, illustrates still another environmental production concept in which audience and performer transactions became organic with the architecture. Here, I turned a large room in New York University's School of the Arts into an environment vaguely reminiscent of a carnival midway. The audience entered an enclosure made up of a collection of antique doors and corrugated metal panels; inside this area the audience could purchase refreshments or view a hexagonal-shaped wooden playing area. This main performer structure was designed to house a literal endgame between two groups, the audience and performers. The audience was seated around the six-sided arena on two levels divided into stall-like cubicles that accommodated two to four people. A companionway

Eugene and Franne Lee: *Candide,* 1974

behind the stalls allowed the audience access into their cubicles. Separating the audience members from performers was a 12-foot-high wire screen which, when lighted properly, prevented the performer from seeing the audience but allowed the audience to see the actors clearly.

In *Makbeth* and *Slave Ship,* the audience had been seated in proscribed clusters on many levels throughout the environment while scenes and transformations took place among them. *Endgame* spectators were situated in cubicles around the performers, suggesting the symmetry and organization of a game board. The audience in the Performance Group's *The Tooth of Crime,* on the other hand, was free to follow the action in an environmental structure whose massive configuration resembled buildings, battlements, streets, rooms, private and public places, heights and the subterranean depths. As I designed it, both performers and audience could use the space or negotiate the use of any part of it with each scene. The space became a cityscape microcosm in which the audience could associate with and follow performers in street-theatre fashion. There developed a real sense of competition for space and vantage points, not unlike the competition about which the play revolves.

A more recent and significantly popular production of *Candide* represents one of Broadway's early environmental efforts. Originating with the Chelsea Theatre and directed by Harold Prince, *Candide* was designed by Eugene and Franne Lee, who collaborated to transform the Broadway Theatre into an environment for a musical comedy extravaganza. This production concept developed associations between the spectacularly prodigious scope of the American musical and the epic, world-wide exploits of the play's protagonist, Candide. The environment encouraged the audience to participate in the medley of chaotic, existential and absurd circumstances of the play, in part because the designers were able to control audience-performer arrangements and flow patterns. For example, aesthetic chaos was created by splitting the normally unified orchestra into various pockets within the environment. And, interestingly, there were essentially two audience groups; one group was directly involved with the production, while the other group circumscribed the main performing areas and, in a way, was watching an environmental production. Using a pastiche of scenic forms the production combined burlesque-style painted backdrops with dynamic set pieces that were carried, flown and mechanized, but were moved in such a way that the audience was able to observe the obvious and ingenious workings of the devices, thereby participating in the openness of the event.

It is interesting to note that environmental designs are not readily translated into pictorial renderings that depict mood or idea. This is because these productions exist in concept which inextricably relies on transactions among audience, performer, text, time and space; the concept is, therefore, perceived internally only during production. Like the layout of a baseball diamond on paper, the environmentalist's models, schematic drawings and ground plans offer a potential that is realized not so much when you consider the color of the grass, but when you consider that a ball travels faster in shallow grass than it does in taller grass.

DESIGNING FOR RESIDENT THEATRES

David Jenkins

On a March evening in 1973 at the Morosco Theatre, Broadway welcomed a new David Storey play, *The Changing Room.* Critical response was favorable; the play went on to win several awards, including the New York Drama Critics Circle Award for Best Play; and Broadway looked a bit brighter. But *The Changing Room* was not having its American premiere; that event had taken place five months earlier, 75 miles to the north in New Haven, Connecticut.

The Long Wharf Theatre, a 441-seat, three-quarter-round theatre sandwiched between a meat-packing warehouse and a commercial printing shop, is the place where this bold play began its American life. No sane Broadway producer would dare touch a play about Rugby football players in North Country, England. But a small resident theatre in Connecticut did and we all benefited.

Bringing a play which has been produced in a resident theatre[1] to Broadway for continuing life is no longer an unusual phenomenon. *The Great White Hope* was originally produced at the Arena Stage in Washington, as were *Indians* and the musical *Raisin. The Trial of the Catonsville Nine* was originally staged by the Center Theatre Group in Los Angeles, while *Solitaire/Double Solitaire,* as well as *The Changing Room,* were first produced at the Long Wharf Theatre. This is, of course, only a partial listing.

While trying to reach some conclusions about the current thrust of theatre in the United States, I became fascinated with these comparative figures: During the 1973-74 season, Broadway produced a total of 46 plays and musicals.[2] At the beginning of 1974, there were 43 professional resident theatres[3] reaching across the country. Assuming the average number of productions for each theatre to be eight, the resident theatre movement unveiled some 345 new productions last year. That's an immense amount of work, and, needless to say, resident theatres provide many opportunities for creative people — actors, directors, designers, playwrights — to gain experience and practice their art. No wonder nearly all the fresh, young thinking of today is found among groups outside the scope of Broadway.

I am a product of the resident theatre movement. My first important job was with the Cincinnati Playhouse in the Park in 1960, its first season. There I gained a great deal of practical experience, not only in design, but in stage carpentry and theatrical construction

David Jenkins: *The Changing Room,* Long Wharf Theatre, 1972

techniques. Following two years in the Army, I spent another season with the Playhouse only to discover that my approach to design for the theatre was one of total naïveté. Therefore I decided to return to academic life, and I chose the Yale School of Drama for study with Donald Oenslager. Once out of Yale, I got a job drafting in a New York scenic studio. But I wasn't designing, and there was little opportunity in New York to break into the work I wanted to do.

Fortunately, I knew Arvin Brown, artistic director of Long Wharf, and he gave me a job designing their production of *The Way of the World.* The domino theory then took effect; I was invited to design at several other resident theatres, including the Arena Stage in Washington, D.C., Goodman Theatre in Chicago, McCarter Theatre in Princeton and Trinity Square Repertory in Providence. If it hadn't been for the resident theatre movement, I could have easily lost interest in stage design.

For 15 years I've been involved with resident theatres, and I've had the opportunity to watch the movement grow. It's been both scorned and heaped with praise; nonetheless, healthy and alive professional theatre in America will never again be thought of as existing only in one or two large urban centers. As a stage designer I find the work for these theatres exciting, meaningful and brimming with creative potential.

Douglas W. Schmidt: *Camino Real*
Cincinnati Playhouse in the Park, 1968

There are problems, of course. Depending on the age, growth and financial status of a particular theatre, various budgetary problems have to be faced. During my first year in Cincinnati, the basic problem was survival. The design budget fell somewhere between the urgent need to buy dressing-room lighting and the necessity for sufficient funds to cover heating costs.

But the overriding theme in all resident theatre experiences is the willingness to take a chance, to fail and fall flat on your face. The pressure for commercial success is off; everyone wants the production to be successful, but that is not the ultimate goal. The management recognizes that where no risks are taken, the project is likely to lack excitement, challenge and innovation. These values, then, take precedence over commercial success. It becomes possible to re-examine scripts that might have fallen short of the mark in a previous production and give them another showing. There is an opportunity to encourage and produce new work by playwrights whose writing might be unknown or too risky for a strictly commercial venture. And there exists the opportunity to revive classic drama and not wait for the star-package or the university production.

For the designer the impact of this philosophy, allowing experimentation and risk-taking, is enormous. There is more opportunity for work than Broadway can provide. There is a willingness to try a new designer, who in New York would likely spend years as an assistant to an already established designer. More important, when the pressure to produce a financial success is removed, the designer can experiment with different techniques and concepts. Without this freedom a designer is liable to fall back on the creative processes he knows have proved successful for him previously. This greatly deters his growth and diminishes the vitality of the work he produces.

In resident theatres there is the constant challenge of designing for new and different spaces. I find it disturbing that it's quite possible to create designs for a Broadway show without ever having to leave your studio. Unfortunately, the audience-stage relationship seldom varies: a 45-foot-wide proscenium opening with terrible sight lines and never enough stage depth. On the other hand, if you ever think about designing for a resident theatre without at least one visit, you are in for some rough times.

I recall that a few years ago I pored over the architectural plans and sectional drawings for the Kreeger Theatre (Arena Stage) and I was sure I understood that particular space. But there was no way to prepare for the jolt I received as I entered from the side door, took a seat, and realized that all of my preliminary work would have to be set aside. The particular problem there, unusual in a theatre seating only about 500, is that the audience in the balcony section sees a much different picture than the audience in the orchestra; the range of viewing angles is enormous for such a small theatre—you don't quite know whom you're designing for.

I have yet to find any two resident theatres with identical audience-stage relationships. Most current trends in audience-stage relationships are represented among the resident theatres: four-sided theatre-in-the-round, unlimited variations of three-sided-seating arrangements, the traditional proscenium-arch configuration, plus open-end seating with no proscenium whatsoever — just space. There is always some quality about each space that will ignite a designer's imagination or, on many occasions, pose problems that require bold and creative solutions in order to serve the specific script requirements.

From the point of view of designers, the variety of theatre spaces encountered throughout the country is beneficial; the designer is not bound to working in one style of theatre. It is my opinion that most designers who work in only one resident theatre tend to stagnate, while those who travel from theatre to theatre grow through the various experiences they encounter.

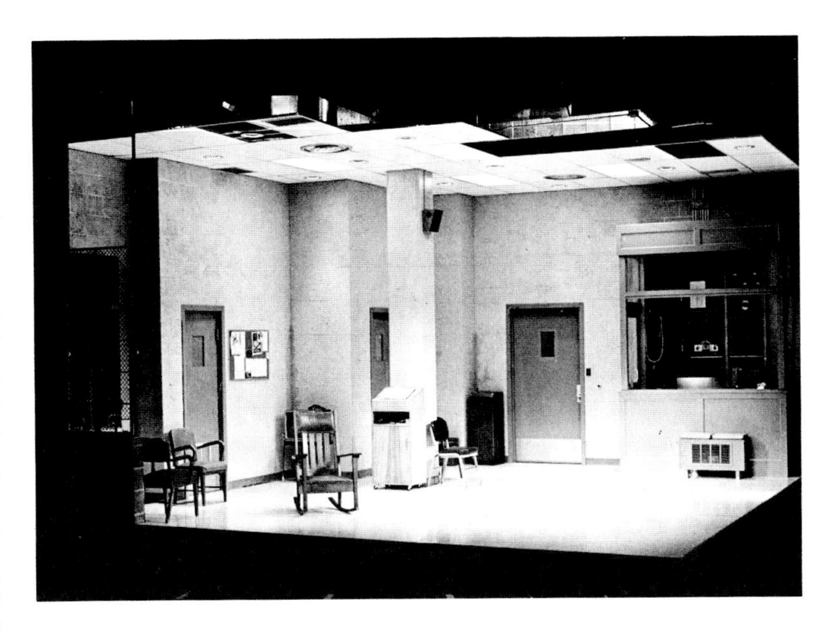

David Jenkins: *One Flew Over the Cuckoo's Nest,* Kreeger Theatre, Arena Stage, 1973

Especially valuable to the designer is the proximity of the scenic shop; in most resident theatres the shop is contained in the same building complex, or at least in the neighborhood. This enables the designer to work closely with the shop staff, thereby encouraging between artist and technician an interplay of ideas which leads to expanded creativity. Because of this close relationship, the craftsmen need not just mechanically execute the drawings, but can become part of the creative process.

Since so many designers pass through various scenic shops, it doesn't take long for a new material or construction method used in Providence, for instance, to reach a shop in San Francisco. Out of this casual arrangement new materials are found, different building techniques are explored, and a wide range of experimentation can exist. Both the designer and the craftsmen are given a chance to develop.

Often the leftovers from a previous show founa around the scenic or prop shops will help solve problems of the current production. As a segment of the design for *Relatively Speaking,* produced at the Kreeger Theatre, I wanted to create an English rock garden. There had to be a way to do it easily, but I wasn't sure how. The shop people knew. An aerosol spray-foam which they had used for another production solved my problem. This process of sharing is reciprocal. I had used a composition board in the construction of deteriorating walls for *The Changing Room* at Long Wharf; it was a material new to the staff at Arena Stage, and I had the opportunity to pass along this knowledge for one of their needs. There is a continuuity among the resident theatres through the shops; ideas don't get lost because the permanent staffs pass them on.

Of course the actual problems of getting the designs executed once the concept has been decided upon vary from theatre to theatre. Some theatres are understaffed, and it is not unusual to find designers with paintbrush in hand. If the designer is there to help, he is usually welcomed into the scenic shop by the technical staff. Most often the designers are directly involved in the making of unusual props or in specialized painting or sculpting on a setting. This direct involvement underlines the fact that stage design remains one of the few handcrafted industries left to our generation.

A danger lurks in the recognition, expansion and growth of resident theatres. There is the possibility that the resident theatre will gradually become so much like the establishment that it will lose some of its daring and creativity. One has to depend on the integrity of the individual managers and directors to maintain the standards and creative approach which have brought them recognition.

Designing for a resident theatre is a unique and exciting experience and easily outstrips the rewards a designer receives from that lumbering cousin known as Broadway. The incredible expansion of the resident theatre movement provides so many opportunities for design. When I left design school and was seeking advice, I was told to find a resident theatre group, join it and design. That rather simplistic approach went straight to the point—go where the work is and work, and you will grow in your work. I have been fortunate, as have been many others, that the resident theatres in the United States have allowed us to do just that.

1. There has been some debate about the use of the terms "regional" or "resident" theatre to best describe the professional groups found outside New York City. Many of them feel "regional" has the connotation of "provincial" or "second-rate." Even though "resident" gives rise to a few erroneous conclusions, I have chosen to be consistent with the current trend and use the term "resident theatre."
2. According to *The New York Times,* June 25, 1974.
3. According to a list of *Theatres Operating under L.O.R.T. Contract,* January 1974, provided by the Foundation for the Extension and Development of the American Professional Theatre.

DESIGNING COSTUMES

Patricia Zipprodt

I have found over the past few years that it is not uncommon for people to believe that all a costume designer does is draw pretty pictures and somehow—maybe they imagine little elves sewing on buttons in the middle of the night—the costumes magically appear on opening night! Well, that's not quite what happens, though sometimes I almost wish it were.

I like to compare the costume sketch to a road map. The sketch, like the map, is not an end in itself; it is a limited guide. In costume design, as in a car trip, the unpredictables of life pop up—the unavailable fabric, the time-consuming detour, the temperamental actor, the flattened tire. The designer and the driver are in a constant state of problem-solving as they travel their respective routes.

How does one prepare these "mini-maps," these sketches?

A thorough analysis of the script is the essential first step. And because the costume designer is a part of a team, there follow conferences between the director and his designers. Actually, I find one of the most satisfying times in the preparation of a new production to be these preliminary meetings, for it is at this time that the overall concept of the work is hammered out. If we consider that there are at least 30 approaches to *Hamlet,* which concept shall we develop as our own on this unique occasion? Each production is unique because it marks the beginning of a new existence.

I look upon theatrical designers as creative extensions of the director; we are the people who make visible the world in which the piece will *live.* If we are working well together, it is because we are working *closely* together. In these discussions we explore verbally and with rough sketches the many different approaches and ideas that might bring the script into dramatic focus on the stage. The designers supplement the concepts of the director visually; in so doing we sometimes have the joyous experience of inspiring the director to the discovery of new ideas. Contrary to popular opinion, the craft of theatre is a collaborative enterprise, not an "ego trip." I recall that while working on *Fiddler on the Roof,* Jerome Robbins, Boris Aronson, Jean Rosenthal and I spent a year working in tandem, exploring innumerable possibilities before rehearsals ever began.

During the preparation of *Pippin,* Bob Fosse, Tony Walton, Jules Fisher and I had a marvelously elastic and comfortable relationship. We spent a summer creating our *Pippin* world without much to base it on in the script. We were unafraid of appearing foolish to one another in presenting ideas which might not be right. We had an extremely difficult time deciding on the right look for the strolling players. The script said, "Enter strolling players of an indeterminate period." Now, to me, this meant exactly nothing. I did a lot of sketches, which everybody seemed to like. On the day I was supposed to present finished sketches, time ran short. Instead of fully coloring the costumes of the strolling players as was planned and expected, I just painted in beige and off-white washes so that Fosse could read the sketches more easily. I put the whole group of 14 or 15 in front of him and was just about to apologize for not getting the color done when he said, "That's just brilliant, exactly the colors they should be. How clever of you!" The minute he said it, I knew he was right. By looking at those off-white costumes, we all recognized who those "strolling players of an indeterminate period" were. The whole show started to come closer into focus.

During the preparation phase, I research in all pertinent ways the period, its people and places, its history and whatever else might relate to the look and mood of the costumes. For *Fiddler* I spent months learning about the clothes and a way of life which had been totally unknown to me. By the time I was ready to sketch, I could call with ease upon a vast amount of deeply absorbed knowledge. I found that I knew almost instinctively what each character should look like.

Where do ideas come from? From any place at all. There was a short-lived play by Archibald MacLeish called *Scratch,* based on *The Devil and Daniel Webster.* The major costume problem was to determine how people who have been buried for 150 years would look when they return to earth from hell. I read the script, talked with the director, rummaged around in my head for ideas, and suddenly remembered a trip I had once taken to Guadalajara, Mexico. In an old cemetery there, because of the limestone in the soil, the bodies had not decomposed, but had instead petrified. There was a catacomb-like underground museum I had visited in which the bodies were displayed sitting or standing around, fully clothed. Their skin had turned a very strange, parched, saffron yellow; they still had hunks of hair and their teeth. It was a very, very weird experience.

Fortunately I had a postcard in my files showing some of the bodies, and as soon as I looked at it, I realized that this was the point from which to start. I began to recall the look of those 18th- and 19th-century coats and collars on overwhelmingly shrunken 18th- and 19th-century bodies: what seemed to be grossly oversized period shoes from which emerged scrawny legs of parchment and bone; some fabrics untouched by age and decay; others like layers of dust, resting precariously but quietly in proper place; laces rotted, buttons survived. All that I tried to capture and put on stage. Where do ideas come from? Well, I don't know what I would have done without that trip to Guadalajara, but something would have come to me. It was my job. It is good to remember that everything that happens to you on any level is always accessible to you, waiting to help you, if you reach for it.

Patricia Zipprodt: *Pippin,* 1972

All this preparation, research, discussion and evolving of ideas, is marvelous and the only way I am comfortable working. But too often, in the commercial theatre especially, you must make your design commitment too early, well in advance of rehearsal, sometimes even before a script is in rehearsal form. The director can restage and the dramatist can rewrite straight on through to opening night. But the physical production is not so quickly or inexpensively rearticulated. So besides being designers, we must be mind readers, crystal-ball gazers, psychoanalysts, and subliminal message-takers—in short, mini-prophets.

To err is *not* human in the theatre; it is to jeopardize your career. Still, the designer is stuck with his preconceived, enthusiastically "okayed" physical objects, called costumes and scenery, which have cost a lot of money and which may end up not working at all with the way the production finally turns out. I liken this problem to the medievalists' preoccupation with the question of how many angels can dance on the head of a pin. I see the finished theatre piece as the pin. When the show is ready to open, will the set designer, costume designer, lighting designer, director, actors, all have landed on the head of the pin? You must have such intuition to know where the director is when you start and where he will be 16 to 20 weeks later.

I have found that one of the greatest challenges to a designer is to keep up with an evolving show—and they all *do* evolve. There was a real crisis, for instance, with the armor for the war ballet in *Pippin.* I had done a series of sketches, had them approved by the director, and put them into work. I always keep a close watch on a show, especially on a musical; and when I saw the ballet Bob Fosse was creating during early rehearsal, I immediately knew that there was nothing those dancers were doing that they could do in the armor I

Patricia Zipprodt: *Scratch,* 1970

above Patricia Zipprodt: *The Blacks,* 1961
below Patricia Zipprodt: *1776,* 1969

had designed for them. They were bending at the middle *a lot,* bending backwards *a lot,* and moving all over in every kind of contortion. I brought the armor maker down to see it, and we knew there were no existing techniques for constructing armor to solve this problem. So we invented a new method. By using a technique of thin layers of latex alternated with layers of cheesecloth in a mold, the armor was built. The dancers could do anything in those costumes, and the bonus was that the whole costume, leotard and armor sewn together, could be washed in cold-water soap. In this instance, I was caught short momentarily, but what finally developed was a far better solution than the original approach.

Returning to my favorite analogy of the costume sketch being like a road map, you get in your car, map in hand, and intend to reach your destination in two hours. But then you hit a detour, have that flat tire, run out of gas and get a speeding ticket—problems that don't appear on the map. The trip a costume takes from the drawing board to the finished product is equally filled with obstacles. Naturally, the first problem you face once the designs have been approved is budgetary. What I do is to call representatives from all the costume houses together and painstakingly go over each sketch. I describe the fabric, the trimming, type of corseting, construction, number of petticoats, etc. And, yes, I have been tape-recorded during these sessions. I've had people come back to me saying, "But you said it didn't *necessarily* have to be made out of pure silk." So I really have to know what I'm talking about.

The producer is in charge of expenditures and, therefore, handles the bids and the negotiations. Bids always come in higher than budget, and I have to try and keep the right house in the negotiations; each costume shop has its specialty, and it could be a disaster for the wrong house to get the show. It usually works out, but not until the producer has a few more grey hairs. On *Pippin* we had a real budget problem. But we solved it by reducing the number of costumes, rather than the amount of money that could be spent on each costume. We eliminated, but we did not reduce the quality, and in a funny way the show profited, since some of its style came from being on a tight budget.

Once the contract is signed, it's time for picking fabrics, trims, etc. I fuss a lot about fabrics. (If the show is a hit, I may be looking at it for five years.) But you do have to decide quickly because there are only about four and a half weeks to get a show together. If the fabrics are late, everything runs late.

Finally, after weeks of dyeing, draping, cutting, fitting, and doing all the things necessary to get a finished costume, there is your first public showing, the moment of truth—the dress rehearsal—when the costumes are worn on stage in front of scenery and under lights. The questions then are: Do they serve the show, can the actors work in their costumes, does the concept hold? With *1776* all went well except for one dress. When the actress appeared on stage, she promptly disappeared. Her hair and the fabric of the dress simply blended with the background, and there was nothing that could be done about it but build a new dress out of a new fabric. It was simply a case of total miscalculation on my part.

More often than not, however, when you've had a good team working together, it all jells. Of course, the show may not play for more than one performance, but at least you know you've done your best and it's been a satisfying experience. From there you move on to the next.

What does annoy me about all the creative effort that goes into a show is that it all vanishes when the production closes. The craftspeople who built the costumes for *Scratch* were geniuses. We started with union suits dyed that awful saffron color, then layered strips of latex, heating it with hairdryers and stretching it, over and over, to make it look like bones coming through skin. All the clothes were made of gauze and linen scrim with big cutout holes of rot . . . just held together with apparently the sheerest of fabric. And when the corpses of the American traitors came up from hell into the eerie lighting amidst the rafters of the huge old New England barn, it was an extraordinary theatre moment.

Much of the credit for this accomplishment must go to the costume shop craftspeople who explored with me and stretched their imaginations and spirits in so doing. We all thought how marvelous it would have been if each of the costumes, along with detailed sets of instructions on our methods—how we handled the rubber latex, samples of fabrics before and after they were dyed and aged, information on the types of paints and glazes used and how many layers and colors of gauzes were used, and so on—could have been given to the many places around the country where the study and construction of costumes go on (Yale, Carnegie-Mellon, the Guthrie, the Museum of the City of New York Theatre Collection, to name a few), so that this information could be spread. There are so many other ways for such innovative methods to be put to use.

But it does not work that way. The costumes were instantly sold to a costume rental house, probably for $25 apiece, and they surely hang on racks, genuinely rotting away this time, in some warehouse out in Long Island City. They represent a "high" time when all of us were trying to go a little further than we had before, but only a few will ever know about it or have access to it.

Maybe someday the myopic economics of the theatre will no longer deprive future designers of all such valuable information, though I have my doubts. Until then, my colleagues and I will try to do our inventive work as best we can. It is worth it because that thirty-first concept of *Hamlet* might be just around the corner . . . or in some similar place.

NOTES ON DESIGNING MUSICALS

Excerpts from a forthcoming book by Boris Aronson

Boris Aronson

Boris Aronson: *Fiddler on the Roof,* model for the wedding scene

With all contemporary theatre, a designer must be reborn with each show, approach each project, not as a continuation of the last, but as virgin territory to be explored. The difference between a play and a musical is the difference between a painting and a poster. Current musicals are not conceived from scratch with the intention of writing a "musical." *Fiddler on the Roof* was an adaptation of short stories by Sholom Aleichem; *Zorba* was an adaptation of a novel by Nikos Kazantzakis; *Cabaret* was an adaptation of *Berlin Stories* by Christopher Isherwood; *A Little Night Music* was suggested by a film by Ingmar Bergman. With a musical, especially an adaptation, the need for newness, freshness, becomes all the more important. You cannot come to it with a ready-made solution.

In order to surprise the audience, you must be able to surprise yourself.

☆ ☆ ☆

Fiddler on the Roof (1964) . . . The title comes from a famous painting by Marc Chagall. He is the one Jewish artist who has painted the *shtetl,* the Jewish village, from memories all his life. Chagall's colorful fantasy—a man flying through the air, head in hand, a fiddler on the roof . . . his love for the homey little things in life, a shoe, a cat, a rooster—is closest to the folk art of Sholom Aleichem's Yiddish tales. Both the director and the producer of *Fiddler* felt this Chagall quality should be used. It was the emotion of Chagall's paintings I tried to incorporate in *Fiddler,* but the show needed to be solved in terms of its own problems.

Sholom Aleichem, in his tales of Tevye the milkman, describes him and his family as forming a circle within the circle of his friends in Anatevka, the town. I used this image as the key to my design of the musical: a small revolving stage inside a large one . . . on these turntables moved the people of Anatevka and their ramshackle dwellings . . . always against backdrops of delicately colored skies or trees. Even within poverty, there was natural beauty . . . a glow coming from life itself.

Chagall will forever paint *Fiddler on the Roof.* He takes Anatevka with him wherever he goes. I only got to do it once.

☆ ☆ ☆

Cabaret (1966) . . . In 1951 I had designed *I Am a Camera,* a play by John Van Druten, based on *Berlin Stories* by Christopher Isherwood. The stories were written during the Nazi regime in Germany. Harold Prince decided to use the same material as the basis for a musical in 1966. I asked him why he wanted to revive that period. He answered that he saw political similarities in what had happened in Germany then and what was happening in America now.

How do you convey this comparison and social commentary to an audience? When the audience entered the theatre, they saw themselves reflected on stage in a huge mirror . . . saying, "Look at yourselves!"

The show was done from beginning to end in cabaret style. By tilting the mirror it became the ceiling within the cabaret reflecting the performers. It emphasized through distortion the intentionally grotesque quality of the cabaret numbers.

☆ ☆ ☆

Zorba (1968) . . . The song opening the musical *Zorba* begins with the line, "Life is what you do . . . while you're waiting to die . . . ." The basic theme of *Zorba* was about Life and Death and the equally strong forces of each. The setting was Greece, but not the pictorial blues and lush greens of the Mediterranean. What set the visual concept for the musical was the brilliance of the whitewashed mountain villages with their deep shadows. I wanted it to look sculptural, handcrafted, strong in texture and contrasts.

The mountains were made of heavy tapestry and knotting. The sky consisted of loosely woven layers of translucent fabrics. Naturally the sunlight had to be part of the locale. A miniature sculptured village which hung against the sky was conceived as a sundial. It was lit so the shadows should mark the time of day.

☆ ☆ ☆

Company (1970) . . . *Company* was based upon a series of vignettes about married life in New York City. Dealing with a physical concept as gigantic as New York, I was faced with a choice in interpretation. The first problem I faced was one of scale.

Against nature, a man counts. Against the ocean, even a bird counts. Against a street in Paris, the human figure counts. But in New York, only a parade counts.

Designing begins with the size of the human body . . . a constant . . . the size of the actor establishes the scale. The environment surrounding the actor serves to *emphasize* . . . to put the actor into focus. Space is created around the performer.

People who live in glass high-risers shouldn't throw stones . . .

above Boris Aronson: *Cabaret,* stage setting
below Boris Aronson: *Zorba,* model

above Boris Aronson: *Company,* production scene
below Boris Aronson: *Follies,* model

that's *Company.* Married life in New York City isn't rocking the afternoon away on a front porch in Maine. In New York people sit in transparent cages. Apartments are like hospitals . . . antiseptic environments without privacy.

I rejected using neon signs or skyscrapers. Take 42nd Street or any other characteristic New York site. It is ridiculous to attempt to make it seem larger or more exciting than it exists in a photograph or on film. In order to clarify to myself people's behavior in the city, I kept a daily record of how many buttons I pushed in the course of a day.

Movement in New York is vertical, horizontal, angular, never casual. In Versailles you bow, in New York you dodge.

The set was conceived basically as a gymnasium for acting. By making a totally mobile unit set you could make the set seem as big as a city street or as intimate as a one-room apartment.

I think of myself as a painter, and *Company* was the first show in over 100 I have designed that hasn't a drop of paint in it. I chose to use steel, chrome and plexiglass. I used projections to represent reflections of the city.

☆ ☆ ☆

Follies (1971) . . . This was a nostalgia play . . . a play about people returning after 30 years to meet at a theatre which is about to be dismantled. The concept in my design was to make the theatre a place that would elicit very touching memories of the grandeur which took place in that environment. I wanted to imagine . . . to *emphasize* that great dramas, tragedies, epics took place . . . the bits and pieces hanging are leftovers from former glamour. I wanted it to be more than just a music hall.

Memories arrive in bits and pieces . . . they're evocative . . . strung together into chains, colored by the imagination. In *Follies* I used these leftovers, these remnants, very purposely. If you see a statue, and a hand is missing, or the nose is broken, it leaves so much more to the imagination than if it were complete. This very lack of closure creates a positive-negative relationship between the missing pieces and the elements that remain. I took full advantage of this duality, this juxtaposition, to try to create an image of a monumental theatre of bygone days.

And then the surprise . . . Loveland . . . Valentines and lace . . . symmetrical, sweet, rosy . . . rising out of the rubble and ruin. A flash of color amidst the doom.

One of the great problems in *Follies* was to design a set which combined the availability of many performing areas, on various levels, and yet maintained visually the picture of an empty stage . . . an entity in itself . . . a whole.

I solved it by creating movement . . . units which would move front, close to the audience for a particular scene, and then disappear into the background, again becoming part of the rubble and decay . . . dead bones scattered around a room . . . coming together to create a form and then returning to bones.

In *Follies* I wanted to pay tribute to the institution of the theatre, as the process of its dismantling is becoming more than a fantasy.

☆ ☆ ☆

A Little Night Music (1973) . . . This musical was based on a film. Whereas *Follies* was lost grandeur, *A Little Night Music* was pure whipped cream. I made no attempt to create the feeling of times gone by . . . this was not a study in period presentation.

For inspiration I drew on the white nights of Scandinavia, for movement and flow in entrances and exits . . . waltz time.

The basic framework of the script asked for a garden. Gardens on stage worry me. "Only God can make a tree." I had a very vivid memory of white-birch groves in Russia . . . birch trees . . . for the color and locale, and because the birch lends itself to the stylization needed to unify the look of the production. The trees were used in the form of screens to create entrances and exits and simultaneously as a method of shifting scenes.

Trees are traditionally painted on gauze. All that does is to create an abundance of wrinkles and effects of moirés. The birch trees in *A Little Night Music* were painted on panels of Lexan, a plexiglass product. There is nothing more old-fashioned than sliding panels, but these units—paint and appliqué on transparency without any visible framing—gave a feeling of grace, freshness and flow. The reflection of the stage lights off the panels increased the theatricality of the effect.

The appearance of a tapestry, a banquet table, an interior *in* the woods created a Surrealistic look.

I think the greatest joy and novelty to the audience was to watch a musical based on flirtation and sex . . . a production where everyone is *dressed* to kill, but doesn't always make a killing.

This was the surprise in *A Little Night Music.*

Boris Aronson: *A Little Night Music,* model

DESIGNING OPERA

Ming Cho Lee

Opera is theatre, but with a difference. It is musical theatre whose primary means of expression is singing. Opera without singing is unthinkable—it isn't opera. Now, anyone who considers singing an idiotic means of communication will probably find opera idiotic as a form of theatre, and should not be allowed near it. Either you love it, or you find it intolerable; there is no middle ground. I happen to love it.

Some people read mystery stories for relaxation; others watch baseball, the Late Late Show, daytime television—all equally idiotic to the uninitiated. I listen to opera recordings. Heaven is when I can compare at leisure, scotch in hand, the same aria sung by five different tenors, or indeed by the same tenor on three different recordings. I torture people with the game of "who is singing?", and my older recordings tend to have ticks in them at the beginning and end of favorite passages. Of all forms of theatre, this is the one I love and live most completely.

H.M. Crayon: *Manon Lescaut,* Act I, 1949

Love aside, the notion that opera deserves as much serious design attention as any play by Pinter, Miller or Williams is very new in this country, and must be credited to some extent to the efforts of Rudolf Bing. Before 1950, the majority of productions at the Metropolitan Opera (and points west) were in the romantic realism style of the 19th-century scenic tradition—painted pictorial scenery. You can still see this by attending a performance of *Manon Lescaut* at the Met, or of other productions almost anywhere between New Jersey and Florida where opera still consists in parading name singers in front of scenery straight from the warehouse of Anthony Stivanello. As late as 1961, when I was the house design assistant at the San Francisco Opera, the management actually contemplated putting together a production of *A Masked Ball* with scenery from Acts 1 and 2 of *Rigoletto* and the forest scene of *Boris Godunov,* all circa 1920. All of us were saved from this infamous act only because it turned out that both *Boris* and *Rigoletto* happened to be in that season's repertory, and we just couldn't get away with it.

Rudolf Bing opened his first season at the Met in 1950 with Margaret Webster's staging of Verdi's *Don Carlo,* then virtually an unknown opera. While the production, and the setting by Rolf Gerard, would perhaps not be considered a masterpiece today, the intent of presenting opera as a total theatre experience was unmistakable. Few can forget the confrontation between King Philip and the Grand Inquisitor (Siepi and Hines), locked in a room of bare white walls, Philip in black and the Grand Inquisitor in his crimson robe. The impact was, and still is, total and shattering. Designing for opera has not been the same since.

This awareness of opera as theatre with dramatic possibilities, however, did not immediately bring forth a new involvement of American theatre professionals. Until recently the record of major American designers working in opera has been spotty at best. You can almost count on one hand the productions designed before the late 1950's by Americans: Simonson's *Ring,* Jones' *Dutchman,* Mielziner's *Emperor Jones,* Oenslager's *Salome.* While I think that the mistrust of American designers and directors by the essentially European-trained impresarios of established institutions was very much responsible for this, I must admit that the American theatre professionals of the period did not approach opera with anything resembling enthusiasm or understanding. To them, opera meant museum, and a foreign museum at that; Broadway, which was going strong with its endless parade of new plays and musicals, was decidedly more exciting. If any of them condescended to work on an opera, it was with the attitude of bringing Broadway know-how and pizzazz to the stilted proceedings.

It was not until the late 1950's or thereabouts that the situation began to improve. Long-playing recordings of complete operas were beginning to appear, creating a more knowledgeable and interested audience across the country. At the same time City Center Opera (later New York City Opera), because of lack of money, was seriously trying to work out a new and different way of producing opera, a simpler and less grandiose approach that sometimes required even more imagination from the production staff and the audience as well. A great many of the productions were not that successful, but some of them, including *The Ballad of Baby Doe* designed by Donald Oenslager and others designed by Will Steven Armstrong, were very much of a breakthrough. By the way, City Center Opera, then as now, religiously used local talent. Opera even invaded Broadway sporadically and briefly with productions of Gian Carlo Menotti's *The Medium, The Saint of Bleecker Street* and *Maria Golovin.* The setting for *Maria Golovin,* designed by Rouben Ter-Arutunian, was considered a design classic.

In Boston in 1957 and 1958, Sarah Caldwell, in conjunction with Boston University, and with designers David Hays and Robert O'Hearn, produced several seasons of opera that aroused a tremendous amount of excitement. Their very fresh approach is still remembered. At the same time, the Washington Opera Society and

above Rolf Gerard: *Don Carlo,* 1950
below Rouben Ter-Arutunian: *Maria Golovin,* 1958

Donald Oenslager: *The Ballad of Baby Doe,* 1956

the Central City Opera Association in their own way were doing a great deal by using young singers rather than stars and putting the extra money into new productions, rather than rented scenery. Then, in 1965, came the Metropolitan Opera National Company, however short-lived, using American singers, designers and directors. Again, the approach was strictly one of total theatre, with great care taken in preparation, and this company traveled across the entire country. By the time the Met produced *Die Frau ohne Schatten* in the fall of 1966, and New York City Opera moved to Lincoln Center with such productions as *Don Rodrigo, Julius Caesar, Manon* and *Mefistofele,* all of which generated tremendous excitement, opera had become an integral part of the American theatre scene. By the same token, American designers were now a proven commodity, and more and more opera jobs were theirs.

On the surface, there is no great mystery about designing for opera. One goes through much the same agonizing process as one would for any other form of theatre. Whatever training is offered at Yale, New York University and other institutions of higher learning is not wasted here, and a bit of Broadway know-how actually does help. But that is not to say there is no difference. For one thing, everything tends to be bigger in opera. What is luxurious for a Broadway musical in terms of space and numbers of people involved is merely chamber size here. Also, most operas were written for the 19th-century proscenium theatre with an orchestra pit separating audience and performers. The physical requirements are so intrinsically part of proscenium theatre that attempts to stage opera in open or arena theatres have been rare and, with few exceptions, not overwhelmingly successful. Finally, opera and dance are perhaps the only forms of American theatre that have consistently operated in a repertory system. While I find that designing for repertory can be difficult, and the limitations the system imposes staggering, it offers continuity and security, both conducive to good work, both missing in the one-show economy of the commercial theatre.

But music and singing are what make opera designing different. The very nature of those two elements demands from the design something extra, something more than mere depiction of a surrounding. To me, music at its best is not literal. It does not concern itself with details of a kitchen sink or a living room couch. Great music, even great program music, never merely describes or illustrates a situation, an emotion or a state of being; it transcends those mundane functions and becomes in itself a state of being. I doubt that purely descriptive music, suitable for films perhaps, would be able to sustain an opera for long. Even librettos taken from great dramas, when put to music which is merely supportive, do not make satisfactory opera. Only when the music transcends the literal boundary of the words, and together they provide a totally new theatrical expression, does opera become truly alive and exciting.

Singing is not a natural method of communication. It is, instead, a heightened form, appropriate only to an equally heightened and emotionally charged situation. Pinteresque dialogue involving lumps of sugar, the perpetual waiting games of Beckett, such logical assertions as "two plus two equal four," are not good operatic material. Song begins only when speech fails, and only through song can the fleeting passion of a moment in life be arrested, expanded and transformed into an enduring reality. Such a theatre—a theatre of song—can never be naturalistic; it demands design that is beyond naturalism.

Even the so-called *verismo* operas *(Bohème, Cavalleria rusticana)* are not realistic in the true sense of the word. Realism in opera merely indicates a starting point: the story is about ordinary people and is generally based in reality. But that extra dimension of the music is always present. It transforms *Bohème,* a sentimental little story of boy-meets-girl, into an ultimate expression of love and parting; while *Cavalleria,* a melodrama of petty jealousy and murder, becomes a Sicilian passion. And when the opera is *Fidelio,* a realistic Spanish prison of the period, however masterfully designed, simply won't do. Ultimately *Fidelio* has little to do with things Spanish or with any particular prison. It is about all prisons. It deals with the very essence of tyranny and despair, and finally of hope and the human spirit itself. The design concept can be nothing less. Anything short of a visual counterpart to the essence of the opera is inadequate and becomes merely window dressing. And Beethoven doesn't need that kind of improvement. Opera designing is, therefore, much more related to concept than to production requirements. It may not be quite such pure design as that for Martha Graham, but it is still miles away from *Last of the Red Hot Lovers.* It brings the designer's work a little closer to its essence: an interpretive art, rather than an art of problem-solving.

In opera I find myself most frequently confronted by the question of whether one should design for the music or for the words. This problem is much less serious in the obvious masterpieces such as *Otello* and *Tristan,* but more so in lesser works where music and words seem to be at odds, as in Verdi's *Macbeth.* French opera with heavy Germanic themes, such as Gounod's *Faust,* is also typical. Then there are those "exotic" operas, *The Girl of the Golden West* and *Lakmé,* for example, with librettos that are often an embarrassment for all.

Ming Cho Lee: *Don Rodrigo,* 1966

Under those circumstances, the choice depends very much on the director and designer. In *Faust*[1] we opted for a design concept somewhat in the style of Brecht, going against the obvious sentimentality of the score, in order to preserve some of the integrity of the story. We also tried to avoid heaviness in design that might overwhelm the music. For *Madama Butterfly*[2] we deliberately countered the coyness of the first act, both music and text, with a cleanly structured setting to emphasize the strength of character inherent in Cio-Cio-San.

I think a designer for opera must have an instinct for the weight of the music and be able to translate this into visual terms. A large, unbroken expanse of space suggests one musical quality. The same space, broken into small areas or patterns, suggests another. A room painted completely in frescoes gives a sense of lightness and airiness, while an elaborately carved and heavily coved space gives a sense of opulence and weight. Different materials also suggest different qualities, reflecting even the sound of the orchestration. Stone suggests the bass instruments; metal, a percussiveness and sharpness; wood is closer to the lighter warmth of the lower strings, whose tones do indeed emerge from a wooden soundbox.

Very recently, Harold Schonberg took me to task for my designs for the Mozart opera, *Idomeneo.*[3] For him, the piece, being neo-classic in style, had to conform to his concept of neo-classic design—ruined temples and the like. Mozart's opera, however, has little to do with ruined temples. The music is clean, pure in line, lean—and my design reflected this. I used a simple, formal arrangement of cantilevered platforms and two-dimensional wire sculptures to give a sense of place: an open terrace, a harbor, a sacred place. In addition to this, the production had projections of primordial natural elements—the sea, storm clouds, a hot, burning sunset—to support the very real human passions with which the opera deals. As long as the visual weight does not violate that of the music, you *can* go against the style—even abstraction for neo-classicism—in favor of other values in the work.

I understand I have a reputation in New York for being willing to give up a Broadway show in order to design opera anywhere. This is certainly not entirely true—and a rumor like that can be very detrimental to one's career if it is too persistent. Exaggerated though it is, like all rumor it has some small basis in fact. I do find that designing for opera gives me the kind of satisfaction I find all too seldom in other forms. I am in the process of devoting a year and a half of my life to the designs for *Boris Godunov* for the Metropolitan Opera. But where else does one find the opportunity to be involved in—perhaps even contribute to—a work of that scope and magnitude, dealing as it does with the soul and spirit of Russia? And if it at all succeeds, we may have bridged a gap in time and space for audiences and for ourselves, and perhaps realized to some extent the very formidable, if awkward, genius of Moussorgsky. What more could a designer ask for?

1. New York City Opera, directed by Frank Corsaro, 1968.
2. Boston Opera Group (later Opera Company of Boston), produced and directed by Sarah Caldwell, 1962, and Metropolitan Opera National Company, directed by Yoshio Aoyama, 1965.
3. Produced by the New York City Opera at the Kennedy Center, Washington, D.C., directed by Gerald Freedman, 1974.

DECOR FOR DANCE

Rouben Ter-Arutunian

Léon Bakst: *Schéhérazade,* 1910

The measure of any successful decor for the dance lies not only in the beauty of the decor itself, but in the fact that its presence, when combined with movement, stimulates a higher visual experience. Decor for dance has a complementary function but it is of fundamental importance to it. Essentially it is the treatment of space where movement happens.

It is a delicate process that leads to the idea for the design of a ballet decor. To some degree the mind is guided by instinct, which feeds upon an affinity for the personality of the choreographer—his way with movement, his response to music, and the specific aim he may have with this work. To a larger degree it is conditioned by a total submission to the musical score; and to an unknown degree it is influenced by chance.

No matter how ingeniously adventurous and original the design through an introduction and presentation of new materials for the stage, it will still adhere to at least one of the four basic principles that comprise the vocabulary of ballet decor: the *classic,* the *romantic,* the *sculptural* and the *decorative* decor.

The first is the *classic* decor where the stage appears simply as a static cube, undisturbed by outside elements; serene, devoid of the designer's imagination, neutral, self-contained, *closed.* The movement unfolds within it, visibly confined by undisguised physical limitations of the stage space. The overall effect is not unlike a goldfish tank framed in black velour, with its precious inhabitants fleetingly appearing and reappearing back and forth, on and off. This kind of "decor-less" decor is often considered to be most suitable for plotless ballets, frequently performed by "costume-less" dancers. Technically this type of decor utilizes a drop cloth of some kind, usually transparent, which is stretched (not always well) across the back of the stage, flooded with light and enclosed on all sides by blackness, except on the floor. The silhouette of the dancers in motion, perceived against the unobstructed wall of airiness, is of compelling clarity—and not lacking in a certain amount of blandness.

The second, the *romantic* decor, is in total contrast with the *closed, classic* stage and operates to a considerable degree on a psychological level. It seems to open the space dramatically outward, away from us into all directions—to expand the stage into the beyond.

This kind of decor often attempts to evoke the infinite, and frequently uses the device of a realistic presentation of specific materials towards the effect of an honestly fabricated illusion. There is never an attempt at a formal *make-believe.* This demanding concept challenges the sensibility, imagination and technical know-how of the designer in his equal partnership with the choreographer and composer—the author-triumvirate of ballet. It is in this context that one thinks of the names of Tchelitchew, Bérard, Clavé and Carzou, and also Bakst. Their work reveals a preoccupation with the concept of the stage as an infinite space, when at the service of dance.

Léon Bakst's *Schéhérazade* (1910) is possibly the most famous and the most beautiful of all ballet decors. Though the work of Bakst is not really typical of *romantic* decor, Bakst nevertheless frequently achieved a combination of three categories of ballet decor *(romantic, sculptural, decorative),* but never as extravagantly balanced as in this, his masterpiece. This decor is *romantic-illusionist* in the total evocation of the exterior and interior subject of the ballet, immediately conveying this through the curves of its "architecture" and the vibrant, sensuous color, enveloping the entire stage, extending it hypnotically beyond. It is also highly *sculptural* through the ingenious composition of the "architectural"detail and the cunning use of perspective affecting the entire space. And it is highly *decorative* just by itself, and frankly *make-believe* through the obvious fact that it is only painted canvas. The fusion of all these elements is completed by a total affinity with the musical score.

The traditional device of two-dimensional, painted scenery was also generally used by Christian Bérard, the greatest stage designer after Bakst, yet his work never gave the impression of *make-believe,* but usually succeeded in producing an illusion of the essence of the ballet—of subject and score. His sensibility for color and painted light combined with an extreme sense of proportion and an ingenious inventiveness in the manipulation of stage machinery and stage properties. He had grace. His decors for the ballets *Symphonie Fantastique* (1936), *Les Forains* (1945), *La Rencontre* (1948) remain unforgettable. The work of Vertès, Lila de Nobili and Oliver Messel captured a similar charm, whereas it was the originality of Antoni Clavé's decor for the Roland Petit ballet *Carmen* which was so striking at the time of the premiere (1949). It used a black void, in which were suspended brilliantly colorful elements, some fragmentary, some more realistic, all highly evocative. The survival of this ballet in the repertory of various companies is to be credited greatly to the decor, as is the success of another Petit ballet, *Le Loup* (1953), with the design by Carzou.

But the most consequential of these remarkable stage designers in pursuit of illusion was Pavel Tchelitchew, the only designer to have introduced a new dimension to stage design—the use of light for its own sake and an extended reliance upon materials responding to light and to movement. He attempted to capture the feeling of the infinite, of radiant air, and to make visible what is not perceptible but can only be sensed. Luminosity, transparence, light and shadow were his favorite means.

The preoccupation with light as the single element of a decor has intrigued me consistently. It was most directly carried out in my design for *Laborintus* (choreography: Glen Tetley; score: Luciano Berio; for the Royal Ballet, Covent Garden, 1972)—a *light-sculpture* created by shafts of light emanating from self-reflecting mirrors in a black void. Manipulated by dancers on the stage floor, the mirrors became part of the choreography and organized the stage space. This aspect also qualified the decor for the third category, the *sculptural.*

Sculptural decor is the truly three-dimensional decor in relation to the total stage space, which appears to be driven forward and outward and then turned back upon itself, so to speak. The choreography is confined by a predetermined anchor point, which need not be in itself three-dimensional, but which is clearly designed to control the entire stage, usually through placement and appearance. Its presence causes various points of tension—some kind of imaginary magnetic field which charges the total stage space, and reaches inward toward this powerful design element. The anchor point involves the dance movement in a deliberate relationship, a dynamic dialogue between decor and choreography.

Isamu Noguchi has been very prominent in the application of this type of stage which echoes the Constructivist stages of the Russian theatre of the early part of this century and consequently the decor by the Russian sculptors Naum Gabo and Antoine Pevsner for the Diaghilev ballet *La Chatte* (1927). In some ways it also relates to Oskar Schlemmer's spatial experiments at the Bauhaus. Noguchi's work found the ideal collaborator in Martha Graham, whose keen intelligence and instinctive understanding for the spatial relationship between a sculptural stage property and dance movement enhanced Noguchi's designs and made them participants in her choreography. The decor for *Seraphic Dialogue* is particularly successful in its self-contained beauty and its dramatic and functional contribution to the choreography. The illusionist evocation of a sacred atmosphere qualifies it also for the category of the *romantic* decor.

The three-dimensional approach to decor is the most fashionable today. I have followed it, when it seemed appropriate, as it has for the choreography of John Butler, Glen Tetley, Paul Taylor and also Jerome Robbins. I like to remember the decor for Tetley's *Ricercare* (1966)—a simply curved *open-enclosure,* white, pristine, shell-like, placed centrally on the stage floor. At the rise of the curtain two dancers recline in it, and return to it occasionally throughout the ballet. But it is not so much through its physical use that this element participates in the ballet. It is the effect of the design: the half-moon-like silhouette radiates imaginary lines, reassembles them back into itself, and extends them through itself further on to the beyond. Though fairly small in size and quietly lyrical in appearance, this form holds the stage—a third partner in the choreography for the two dancers.

The fourth approach, the *decorative* decor, has always been the most prominent solution to decor for dance. In spite of the collaboration of the *easel painter* during the time of Diaghilev, the treatment of the stage remained fairly unchanged and basically within the tradition of stage design. The aim: to decorate and to give an identity to the stage. The master of all: Bakst, together with Alexandre Benois, Gontcharova, and Picasso, Dali, Rouault, Berman and Chagall. This approach to decor, which is mostly two-dimensional and based on painted canvas in a pursuit of formal *make-believe,* has currently come to be regarded as terribly old-fashioned—not to a small extent for being extremely time- and skill-consuming in both design and execution. It is most often used in "ballet spectaculars"—innumerable *Nutcrackers, Sleeping Beauties, Coppélias* and *Swan Lakes*—for reasons superficially referred to as "public taste"—beloved by audiences young and old since time immemorial.

It is the designer's artistic sensibility which determines the appearance of the decor—or is it? The collaboration with the choreographer is a major influence upon the work of the designer,—and vice versa,—in friendly retaliation. Another facet is company policy, that is, the purpose for the production of a certain ballet at a particular time in regard to repertory, ensemble, box office, and touring. Producing a full-evening bread-and-butter ballet spectacle at considerable cost, any company would be ill-advised to indulge in an experimental approach, although this might be hoped for and expected from a work of short length set to a contemporary score. In accepting a commission it is not inappropriate for the artist-designer to consider these factors.

Finally there is no one other than the designer who through his talent can shape the appearance of the decor, whatever the approach, the demands and the frustrations, and who sometimes, when blessed, can succeed in presenting a visual counterpoint to sound and movement.

Isamu Noguchi: *Seraphic Dialogue,* 1955

Rouben Ter-Arutunian: *Ricercare,* American Ballet Theatre, 1966

TRAINING THE STAGE DESIGNER

Charles Elson

Fifty years ago, the concerned and visionary in the American theatre were becoming aware that our classic theatre training grounds had all but disappeared under the impact of the phenomenal growth and broadening appeal of the cinema. Our institutional theatres, the stock and repertory houses, with their capacity to train, instruct and provide practice and experience, had virtually been closed by this competition. Our free enterprise system and the absence of available public funds eliminated the alternative of government subsidy of theatre schools, so it was logical to make use of our existing educational system for training theatre students. George Pierce Baker, a pioneer in using the university for this purpose, established in 1912 courses and a workshop at Harvard for playwriting and the newly recognized discipline of stage direction. In 1914, Pittsburgh's Carnegie Institute of Technology inaugurated an undergraduate program with emphasis on acting. Finally in 1926, the stage was set for a school encompassing all the arts and crafts of the theatre with the founding of the professionally oriented Graduate School of Drama at Yale under Mr. Baker's direction.

In considering the training of the stage designer, it should be noted that the function of that artist had, early in the century, gone through a metamorphosis. Essentially, the scenic artist, with only a rough knowledge of setting the stage, was concerned solely with painting; his training consisted of an apprenticeship in a scenic studio. The impact of the new imperative to achieve synthesized productions under the aegis of the director, as total coordinator of the arts of production, made for a concept of the stage designer as a collaborative, interpretive artist with full responsibility for all the visual elements and the technology involved. In Europe, young designers matured from their apprenticeships under the designer-maestros of the institutional theatres or from their subsequent studies in academies. In the U.S., the entire groundwork for this new discipline and its teaching had to be developed. Beyond the European publications concerned with philosophical attitudes, technical advances and reproductions of settings, there was no specific body of organic knowledge dealing with this area of training until 1925-26 when Donald Oenslager in stage design and Stanley McCandless in stage lighting codified, in their Yale lectures and demonstrations, an educational approach. Their approach became the model for the discipline, which, through their disciples, quickly spread nationwide to other academic centers. In the ensuing 50 years, comprehensive theatre curricula have been established and are now flourishing at 1,024 of our universities and colleges—a striking illustration of the recognition and acceptance of this young discipline by the bastions of academia. With their present complexes of theatre structures, these institutions attempt to fulfill their function as our primary training ground for stage designers.

How do we generally go about training and nurturing our neophytes in stage design? The majority of them are exposed to the elementary undergraduate courses of study in liberal arts and humanities programs. Generally permitting only 24 to 36 credits in theatre (about one quarter of the total academic requirement), the program usually exposes students to two stage design courses, one or two costume, lighting and technical courses, plus classes in directing, theatre history, play analysis, dramatic literature, and the production workshop where the enthusiast spends unlimited time. This Bachelor of Arts program is essentially one of enrichment, and most of the students do not contemplate a life devoted to theatre. Those who do, under the circumstances, must elect to go on to intensive graduate work.

The serious undergraduate students, however, enroll, where they can, in a Bachelor of Fine Arts course of study which requires them to take half their credits in theatre and associated arts, and which concludes with a senior project. These students are exposed to advanced design instruction and heavier production responsibilities. The B.F.A. at Carnegie-Mellon, essentially our only professionally oriented undergraduate program, requires a four-year theatre-and-art concentration with a minimal one tenth of the total credits in the humanities. In this intensive study, there are available six scene design, six costume design and four lighting design courses; there are four technical production sections, plus courses in directing, rendering techniques, art and history. In addition, there are four years of production workshops, and the degree requirement includes designing a thesis or major production. Candidates in such a program are thoroughly grounded in their specialty. To insure the quality of the talent accepted, Carnegie stringently interviews each design candidate and accepts only ten out of 40 or 50 applicants—a unique practice among undergraduate institutions.

Despite its obvious value, such an undergraduate program in stage design does raise inevitable questions. Can this B.F.A. degree produce an all-around human being and artist with a keen appreciation of what goes on in our culture? What happens to the sensitivities that must respond to the subtle interpretations that bring out the essence of dramatic literature? Isn't genuine creativity stifled without a thorough grounding in the liberal arts?

The B.F.A. degree, then, offers the student the most intensive training in stage design on the undergraduate level. However, since an undergraduate degree will not generally find them employment, the most determined students go on to a Master of Fine Arts program, coupling this training with summer experience in stock, musical or dinner theatres. The finishing schools for designers are the M.F.A. programs that exist in our major universities. Smaller classes, a higher level of instruction and criticism, coupled with a heavier production schedule and consequently more design responsibility, culminate in a comprehensive design thesis project or production, which encompasses all the visual elements of the chosen script. If there is a professionally oriented training ground in academia, this should be it. In my opinion, Yale University, which once brought to its faculty articulate master teachers, has recently been superseded by at least eight other graduate departments (among them, New York University, Brandeis, Southern Methodist University), which, having acquired renowned designers, are beginning to achieve quality results.

Of the total 750 scenic designers who hold membership in the New York Local of the United Scenic Artists (which, incidentally, doesn't guarantee employment), two thirds are products of the academic theatre. Others come from art and architectural backgrounds, and at least 140 come from the only non-degree professional design academy, the Polakov Studio & Forum of Stage Design in New York City. At this point, one should answer the question: how and where do these many trained designers find an outlet for their specialized art? They obviously all don't achieve their aspirations. Some work on Broadway and Off Broadway. Others are resident designers in the approximately 45 regional theatres, in winter and summer stock theatres, in the cinema and TV. A large number remain as teachers and designers in the university theatre. Still others find their way into the related art fields of architecture, interior design, architectural lighting, advertising, displays, fashion shows. Needless to say, many designers practice their art as an

Carnegie-Mellon University: *Tango,*
directed by Sirin Devrim, settings designed by Thomas Travix Mercer, costumes designed by Anne Wolff, lighting designed by Sander Gossard, 1971

avocation in their communities where at least 200,000 organizations produce plays for local audiences.

While the university training system produces designers who may or may not find employment in theatre or related arts, what about the quality of that training? The most publicized estimates of the achievements and failures of the academic theatre departments have come from our European confreres. In the mid-1960's, Michel Saint-Denis, on his tour of our teaching centers, analyzing actor training and searching for a definitive approach that he could recommend to the Juilliard School, indicated that invariably the visual productions witnessed were, in his judgment, excellent and generally superior in concept and execution to the performers' and directors' contribution. University productions with their glorious visualizations, minor miracles of inventiveness, are often hollow, and the settings usually succeed in standing in front of the performers rather than in the same plane. This dichotomy seems to point up the necessity of improving our training of actors and directors, and of bringing about a closer relationship between the training of the designer and the director.

Carnegie-Mellon University: *Volpone*,
directed by Lawrence Carra, setting designed by Steven Graham,
costumes designed by Arnold Levine, lighting designed by
Leo Bonamy, 1971

There is, it seems to me, a general failure or inability on the part of directors to accept the responsibility of projecting conceptual approaches. Josef Svoboda expresses his "concern with the need of intense and intimate co-creative work between the director and designer-scenographer towards the creation of a scenario that delineates the total production concept, a scenario in which the playscript, the direction, and the scenography are mutually reinforcing elements. It is a team effort in which the director is aware of the ways in which scenography can help express his vision of the play and in which the designer-scenographer is actually involved in embodying the director's production concept." Our theatre is woefully lacking in directors who can inspire designers with a stimulating initial concept. Rarely does the director provide perceptive guidance towards a specific, imaginative, contemporary approach to the interpretation of the playscript. Too often the dramatic image originates with the designer. This leads on Broadway and elsewhere to a succession of presentations that are triumphs of production over content.

This critical problem should be resolved in the training of directors by exposing them to specific visual-element instruction that makes them "aware of the ways in which scenography can help express their vision of the play"; that gives them the means and vocabulary to articulate to a designer their specific conceptual approach. The director must have the sensitivity and knowledge to arrive at a special vision. For this he must be submerged in all the

Carnegie-Mellon University: *Situation Comedy*,
direrted by Lawrence Carra, settings designed by Warner Blake,
costumes designed by Judith Hudson, lighting designed by
Michael J. Garl, 1971

arts and be made aware of what energizes our contemporary culture. The leader of the team must be the director, and achievement in the theatre rests upon his ability to accept this responsibility.

In a similar way the American designer emasculates his ability to realize his total creative concept when he delegates the art and task of lighting that concept to a lighting designer. The ambience of any setting must be conceived in light that is inherent to the total design. Our stage designers must be capable of personally achieving their total visions.

Considering the large number of functioning stage designers in this country, we can be encouraged by the high level of talent exhibited. The training system has had positive results, often turning up genius that is distinctly original. But there is room for improvement. The endeavor to produce future designers of significant talent for our national theatre is essentially dependent upon the upgrading of the university programs. I am convinced that the numbers of aspiring candidates should be sharply weeded, and that the total artist should be the product of an elite atelier-schooling where the master artist-teachers are intimately aware of the progress of their students. In his remarkable 45-year residency at Yale, Donald Oenslager developed only some 250 designers. Carnegie-Mellon's system of accepting a limited number of applicants in each category in its M.F.A. program is ideal. As Ned Bowman of the University of Pittsburgh observes, "Our egalitarian education system allows a lot of unqualified students to enter design programs, and too many of these graduate even though they can't design."

One takes it for granted that it is important to steep designers in dramatic literature, play analysis and a thorough knowledge of the needs of directors and actors. What is further required is that faculty designers radically reduce the number of productions they design in their institutions in order to provide maximum exposure of students to realized work. Endless unrealized projects can be stultifying. The academic disease of proliferating courses that reiterate must cease, and the program of study must be tightened up. Furthermore, there must be a bearing-down on the attitude of the bigger the better; there must be a strong effort to return to the credo of maximum results from minimal efforts. Above all, there must be an attempt to encourage the intuitive and a deep feeling for the place of design in the total production.

THE NEW INTERNATIONAL DESIGNER
or
"Have Sketches, Will Travel"

Eldon Elder

There is a special significance in this book on U.S. stage design and in the exhibition which it catalogues. It lies, I believe, in the recent reversal in the thinking of practicing designers in the U.S. today. Until very recently we looked to Europe—to the Old World—for leadership, for inspiration, perhaps even for ideas to swipe. Rarely, if at all, did it occur to us that *we* might have ideas and techniques of value for designers around the world. I stoutly maintain that the American designer today has, to borrow the words of Edward Gordon Craig, ". . . a nimble inventiveness, a firm independence and a style of his own." Perhaps this view of our own worth was crystallized for us in the disappointment our foreign colleagues expressed when the U.S. failed to exhibit at the Prague Quadrennials in 1967 and 1971. Their looks seemed to say: "Your American musicals are great, your plays by Eugene O'Neill, Arthur Miller, Tennessee Williams, Neil Simon and others are so richly American. How have you, the American designers, mounted them? We want to see what you have been doing. Here is our contribution; where is yours?"

Time was when young American designers, like all aspiring, self-respecting artists, took a year abroad as a part of their education and cultural exposure. Robert Edmond Jones did it; so did Lee Simonson and Donald Oenslager. But once back on native shores, these designers seldom, if ever, returned to Europe to work. Contemporary Stage Design—U.S.A. heralds our international coming of age, I think, by enabling theatre people throughout the world to see what we are doing, and by opening the door a bit wider to the possibility for work by American designers abroad.

For a long time European designers have enjoyed the advantage of working internationally. Undoubtedly, the proximity of countries in Europe has facilitated this fruitful exchange of artists. U.S. designers have been a little slow in arriving on the international scene, but in recent years the pace has accelerated. It took an internal upheaval, both geographic and artistic, to make the U.S. designer realize that he can work abroad as easily as he can in California, that his working season can comprise productions in New York, California, Texas and Minnesota. The distances involved are the same as those between London, Moscow, Istanbul and Tel Aviv; only in the Soviet Union could a designer cover as much territory while working within his own country.

In part it was the diminishing Broadway marketplace, where only a few years ago a number of designers could have been guaranteed season after season of work, that encouraged and even forced American designers to stretch their working base over a broader area. The rapidly expanding regional theatre movement provided new opportunities to U.S. designers to work in a greater variety of theatres and be involved in a greater variety of theatre experiences. Also, the growing number of opera and dance productions increased the designer's scope. These diverse experiences have better prepared the American designer to join the international theatre scene.

It is happening. Jet planes, instant world-wide communication, the European Economic Community, international agreements, foreign tryouts, government-sponsored exchanges are all encouraging the evolution of a new breed of international designer who can travel around the world to design everywhere with as much ease as the Bibiena Family moved through Europe in the 18th century. "Have sketches, will travel!" is becoming the slogan of the new international designer.

The evidence is already there: Josef Svoboda's designs can be seen not only in Prague, but in London, on Broadway, at the Metropolitan Opera House, and doubtless, in a dozen other theatre centers around the world. British designer John Bury frequently designs on Broadway, while U.S. designers David Mitchell and José Varona work at the Paris Opera, and Ming Cho Lee's designs can be seen in London and Argentina.

Unquestionably there are many forces conspiring against this internationalism. There are the political barriers, the ethnic and language barriers, the need for work permits, negotiations with foot-dragging government agencies, cautious trade unions and short-sighted professional societies. Once a foreign designer is contracted to a job, he faces more specific obstacles. In each country there are different methods of work as well as varying attitudes and priorities. In some European countries the two-hour lunch takes priority over work. Quitting time is *quitting time* no matter how overwhelming the crisis. Delayed openings are not uncommon. On the other hand, the *bête noir* for all designers working in the United States is "overtime." Recently, while doing *Will Rogers' USA* for Broadway, it struck me that, in the eyes of the producer, the achievement of setting and lighting the production within one eight-hour call (no overtime) was of more significance than the fact that the scenery and lighting were well designed.

Perhaps the most common problem an American designer working in Europe faces, after the language problem, is dealing with the conversion of feet into meters. Translating from one standard of measurement to another can prove perplexing at the start. It is difficult, like a foreign language, until you have mastered it well enough to "think" in the other system. For myself, I admit that I still visualize in feet and inches and then make the translation. More fluency will come with practice no doubt.

The designer's responsibilities are not the same in all countries. In Italy, Germany and many other European countries where theatre is an institution, the House provides design technicians. The designer's responsibility may end once he has delivered sketches, a model and rough plan to the technicians. The work is done in the shop attached to the theatre, and in the best theatres there is great pride in the craftsmanship and expertise. There is even resentment and resistance if the designer snoops around, "interfering" with the execution of his designs. American designers have experienced this abroad and have had to adjust. Since we do not have theatre as an institution in the U.S., we have grown accustomed to working and following through in great detail simply because there is no one else to do it.

Often foreign designers come here to work and, except at the Metropolitan Opera, find themselves in deep trouble. They are at the mercy of a contractor who, quite naturally, is hoping to turn a profit. The contractor must deliver so much scenery for such and such a price and has no support staff or budget to assist the designer. Foreign designers who have worked in New York have varying reactions to the working conditions with which they are faced. They are frequently appalled by the inadequacies of our Broadway theatres, but they are amazed at the expertise of our technicians. There is "a kind of energy in New York," they say, a "Yankee know-how" that gives Broadway shows the gloss and glimmer and sheen for which they are famous and which seem to exist nowhere else in the world. There is also a pride in the work, they say, which is unique and more than just a reflection of the hefty paycheck that the American technician takes home each week.

Conversely, because the state-subsidized designers working in state-operated theatres of Europe are able to experiment, they are showing the way, in many cases, in the development of new equipment and techniques. Siemen's laser light is beyond our means, for example. It is at present commercially unfeasible. Projectors and projection techniques in Germany and Czechoslovakia are more experimental and consequently more advanced than ours.

Around the world there are different approaches to work: scale models vs. technical drawings, colored model vs. scaled color elevations, repertory vs. the straight run, thrust experience vs. proscenium experience. Josef Svoboda has acknowledged that his training was limited to the proscenium and that he feels less at home working on the arena or thrust stage. And in America we have bred a generation of designers many of whom have totally missed the proscenium experience and are limited in the opposite direction. Another difference concerns the approach to lighting. The work of a lighting designer, as we define the job, is still almost unknown in Europe. England has, under Richard Pilbrow's Theatre Projects Ltd. and Frederick Bentham, developed and promoted the concept recently.

In addition to the practical problems designers encounter in foreign countries, it has been suggested that one danger facing a movement toward the internationalization of designers would be a loss of national identity, of national personality, style or historic heritage. I disagree. Those aspects of a designer's work which are uniquely associated with his heritage have been solidly imbued in him through his early native training as an artist, and through constant exposure to the daily life, the art, the artifacts and the style of his country.

Recently there has been a spate of revivals of American "classics" in London's West End. Invariably the design has been disappointing. The British designer, totally competent in his craft, has presented the American scene from a Hulton-Radio-Times-Picture-Collection knowledge which lacks the deep experience and understanding that is necessary to make it authentic—not factually authentic, but emotionally, aesthetically, tactually and stylistically authentic. How much better to have invited those London designers to the U.S. to design Congreve or Shaw while bringing Americans to London to lend verisimilitude to productions of American plays.

For an audience viewing a foreign play, the design is one of the readily accessible aspects of the production. *Inherit the Wind* may mean little to an audience in Moscow. The audience may be baffled by the foreign language, disagree with the morals, the ideology or the politics of the production, but it can comprehend and appreciate the design it sees. The understanding of another culture is enhanced and clarified by the design images that delight and inform the spectator's eye.

Not to be discounted in a discussion of designers working internationally are the financial benefits made possible by world-wide exposure. When a designer has lent his talent to making a success in one country, it is my belief that he should have the right to profit from that success if the work is reproduced elsewhere. In discussing productions of his work abroad, even Gordon Craig admitted to "having the ordinary British desire . . . to profit a little, too." Parenthetically, it is of interest that in the United States the actual designs remain the property of the artist; elsewhere they usually become the property of the theatre. It is also worth noting that while European designers are envious of the *seemingly* enormous fees paid to Broadway designers, the American designer envies the European who has a staff of assistants and technicians hired by his theatre or his government at no expense to him, enabling him to design more and experiment more.

And yet, with all the differences, when designers are united at international meetings, colloquiums and exhibitions, the shoptalk confirms the remarkable similarities among work methods and conditions, motivations and goals. What stands out and is most striking, nation to nation, theatre to theatre, are the many similarities. The similarities are on the increase—the differences on the decline. Eventually the similarities will demolish the barriers.

PLATES

FOLLIES
by Sondheim and Goldman
Winter Garden, New York City, 1971
Model of set design

CHILDREN OF FAITH
Dance, music by Paul Hindemith and choreography by Renate Schottelius
Dance Theatre of the Boston Conservatory of Music, Boston, Massachusetts, 1973
Sukey (Pas de deux)

MAN OF LA MANCHA
by Wasserman, Leigh and Darion
ANTA Washington Square Theatre, New York City, 1965

THE WAY OF THE WORLD
by William Congreve, Project, 1972
Act III

BRAIN
by Maxine Klein
Boston University Theatre, Boston, Massachusetts, 1972
Rendering of set and environment as viewed from rear of orchestra level

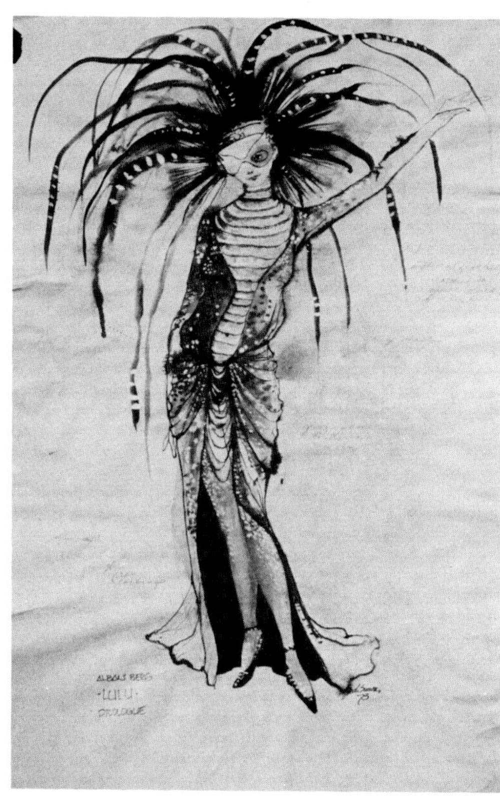

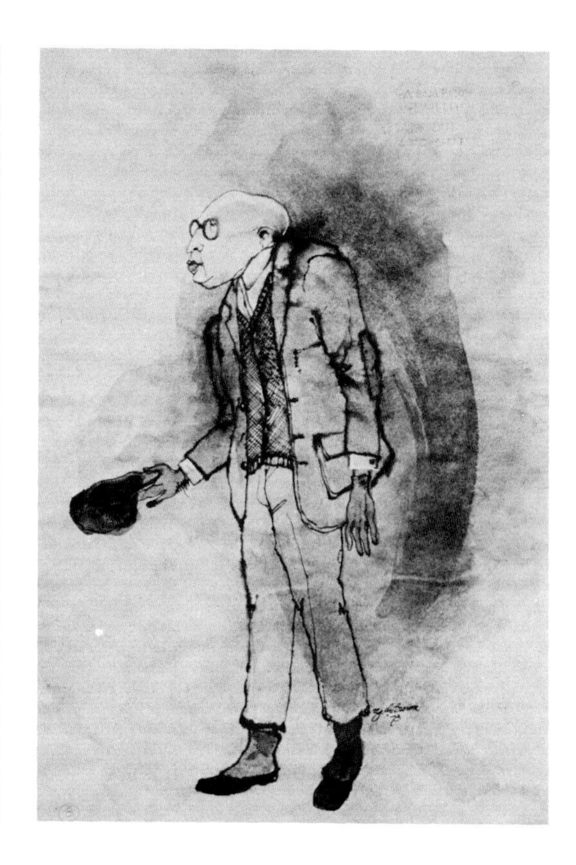

LULU
by Alban Berg, Project, 1973
left Animal Tamer (Prologue) *center* Lulu (Prologue) *right* Schigolch (Act I, Scene 2)

HALLOWEEN
by Leigh and Michaels
Florida State University Theatre, Tallahassee, Florida, 1972
Projection design for the haunted house

RODELINDA
by George Frederick Handel
Holland Festival, 1973
Model of set design (Act I, Scene 2)

HENRY V
by William Shakespeare
American Shakespeare Festival, Stratford, Connecticut, 1969
left Constable of France *right* King of France

THE MAKROPOULOS AFFAIR
by Leoš Janáček
New York City Opera, New York City, 1970
left Emilia Marty (Act I) *right* Elina Makropoulos (Prologue)

THE HOSTAGE
by Brendan Behan
Arena Stage, Washington, D.C., 1972
Model of set design

THE LOWER DEPTHS
by Maxim Gorky, Project, 1973
from left to right Pepel, Luka, Anna Kleshch, Andrei Kleshch, The Actor, Bubnov, Satin, Kvashnya, The Baron

WARP
by Bury St. Edmund and Stuart Gordon
Ambassador Theatre, New York City, 1973
Valaria, Insect Sorceress (Act I)

TOSCA
by Giacomo Puccini
University of Wisconsin, Madison, Wisconsin, 1972
left Tosca (Act II) *right* Scarpia (Act I)

THE VISIT OF THE OLD LADY
Opera by Gottfried von Einem
San Francisco Opera, San Francisco, California, 1972
Railroad station

TROILUS AND CRESSIDA
by William Shakespeare
Shakespeare Summer Festival, Washington, D.C., 1972
Death of Hector

TREEMONISHA
Opera by Scott Joplin
Wolf Trap Farm Park for the Performing Arts, Vienna, Virginia, 1972
left Treemonisha *right* Zodzetrick

MAME
by Lawrence, Lee and Herman
Winter Garden, New York City, 1966
Literary period

KARL EIGSTI

THE KARL MARX PLAY
by Rochelle Owens
American Place Theatre, New York City, 1973
Finale

PANTAGLEIZE
Opera by Robert Starer
Brooklyn College Opera Theatre, Brooklyn, New York, 1973
Promenade

ROSMERSHOLM
by Henrik Ibsen
University of Massachusetts, Amherst, Massachusetts, 1974

THE THREEPENNY OPERA
by Brecht and Weill
University of Hawaii, Honolulu, Hawaii, 1973
Tiger Brown

CANDIDE
by Bernstein and Hellman, Project, 1968
Marketplace

MACBETH
by William Shakespeare
University of Massachusetts, Amherst, Massachusetts, 1973
left Thanes' ceremonial robes *right* Lady Macbeth (Act I, Scene 6)

ANTIGONE
by Jean Anouilh
American Shakespeare Festival, Stratford, Connecticut, 1967

THE RULING CLASS
by Peter Barnes
Goodman Theatre, Chicago, Illinois, 1972

ROMEO AND JULIET
by William Shakespeare
Shakespeare Summer Festival, Washington, D.C., 1968
left Mercutio at the Mardi Gras (Act II)   *right* Paris (Act III)

THE BOYS IN THE BAND
by Mart Crowley
Theatre Four, New York City, 1968

THE CHANGING ROOM
by David Storey
Morosco Theatre, New York City, 1973
Model of set design

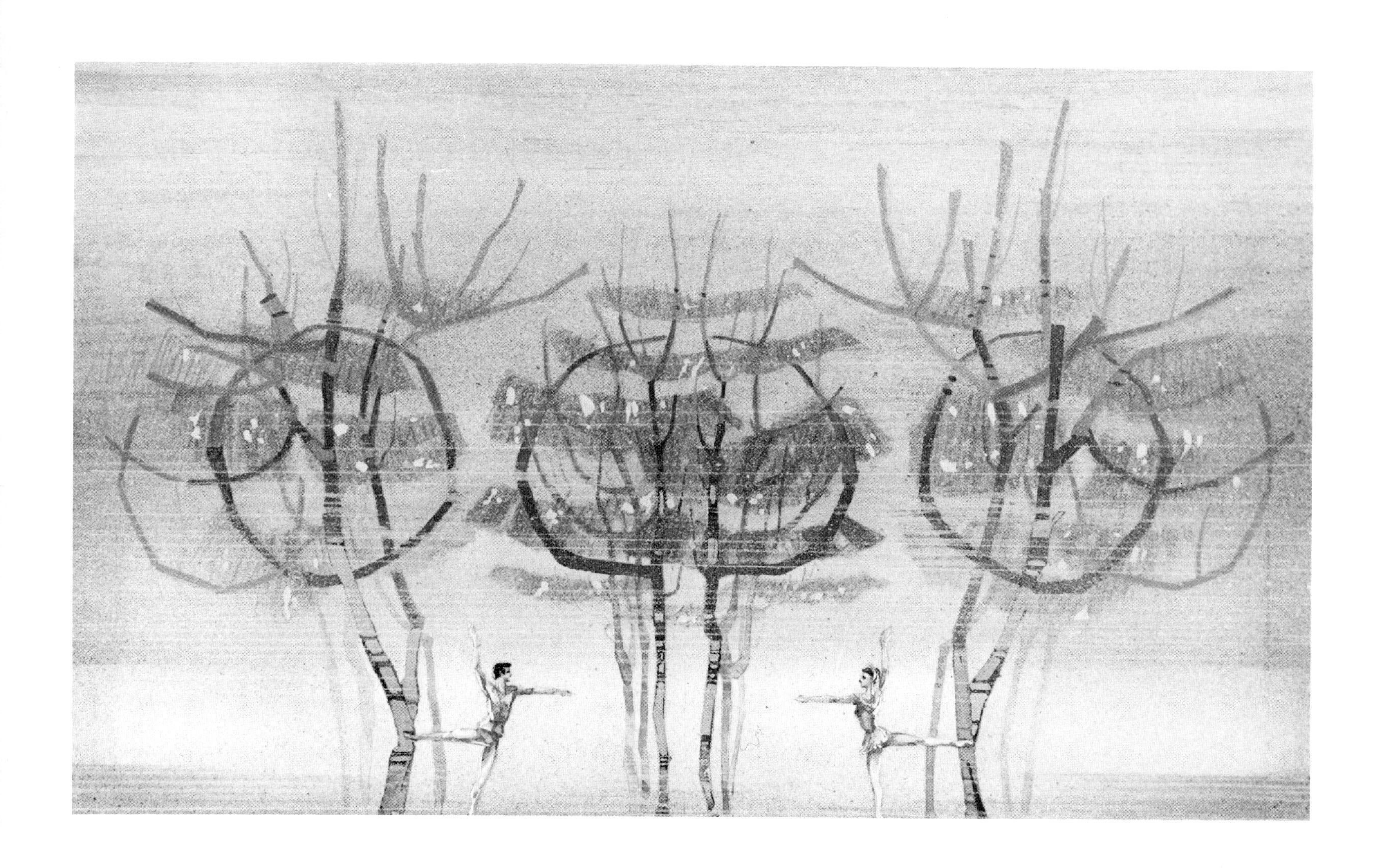

BARTÓK PIANO CONCERTO NUMBER 3
Ballet, music by Béla Bartók and choreography by Ben Stevenson
Harkness Youth Dancers, 1970
Pas de deux

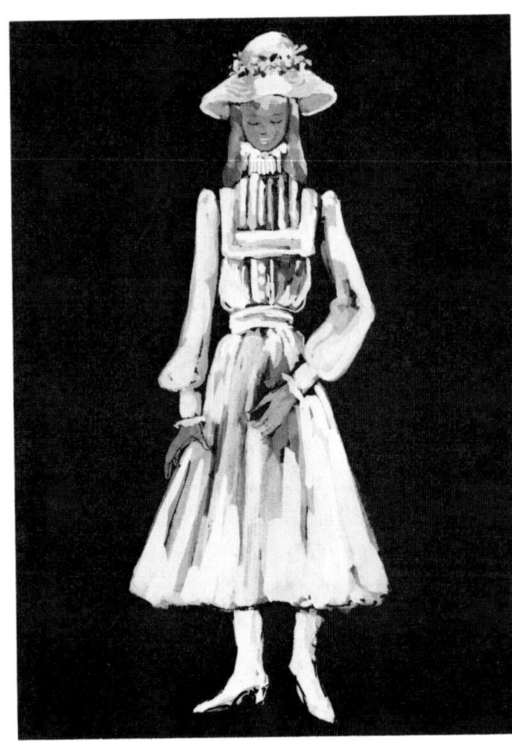

A LITTLE NIGHT MUSIC
by Sondheim and Wheeler
Shubert Theatre, New York City, 1973
left Mme. Armfeldt *center* Fredrika *right* Desiree

CABARET
by Masteroff, Kander and Ebb
Brunswick Music Theatre, Brunswick, Maine, 1971
Kit Kat Klub

SEBASTIAN
Ballet, music by Gian Carlo Menotti and choreography by Vicente Nebrada
Harkness Ballet, New York City, 1974

MUCH ADO ABOUT NOTHING
by William Shakespeare
Delacorte Theatre, New York City, 1972
Model of set design

BORIS GODUNOV
by Modest Moussorgsky
Metropolitan Opera, New York City, 1974
Model of set design

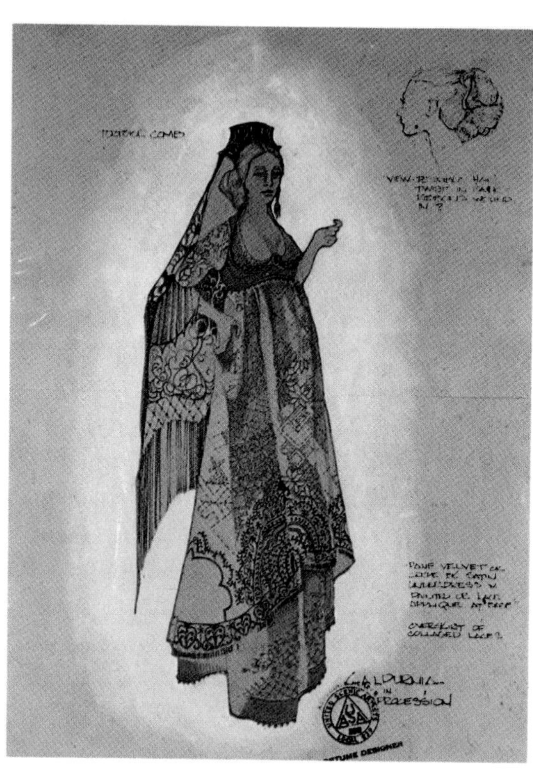

JULIUS CAESAR
by William Shakespeare
Guthrie Theatre, Minneapolis, Minnesota, 1969
left Caesar *center* Calpurnia *right* Lady Citizens

AMAZING GRACE
by Studs Terkel
University of Michigan, Professional Theatre Program, Ann Arbor, Michigan, 1967

PATTON CAMPBELL

THE MAKROPOULOS AFFAIR
by Leoš Janáček
New York City Opera, New York City, 1970
Emilia Marty (Act III)

MABEL ASTARLOA

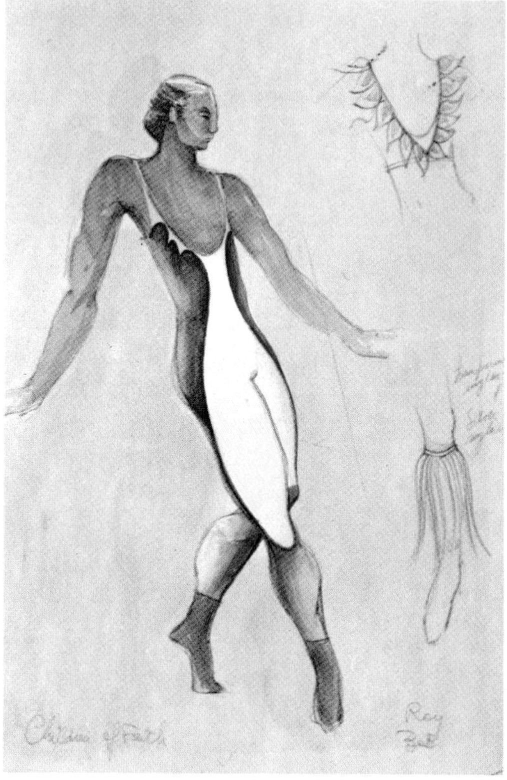

CHILDREN OF FAITH
Dance, music by Paul Hindemith and
choreography by Renate Schottelius
Dance Theatre of the Boston Conservatory
of Music, Boston, Massachusetts, 1973
Roy (Pas de deux)

LAURA CROW

WARP
by Bury St. Edmund and Stuart Gordon
Ambassador Theatre, New York City, 1973
Chaos, Prince of Madness (Act II)

ARCO-IRIS
by Murillo Neri
Teatro Republica, Rio de Janeiro, Brazil, 1968
Curtain

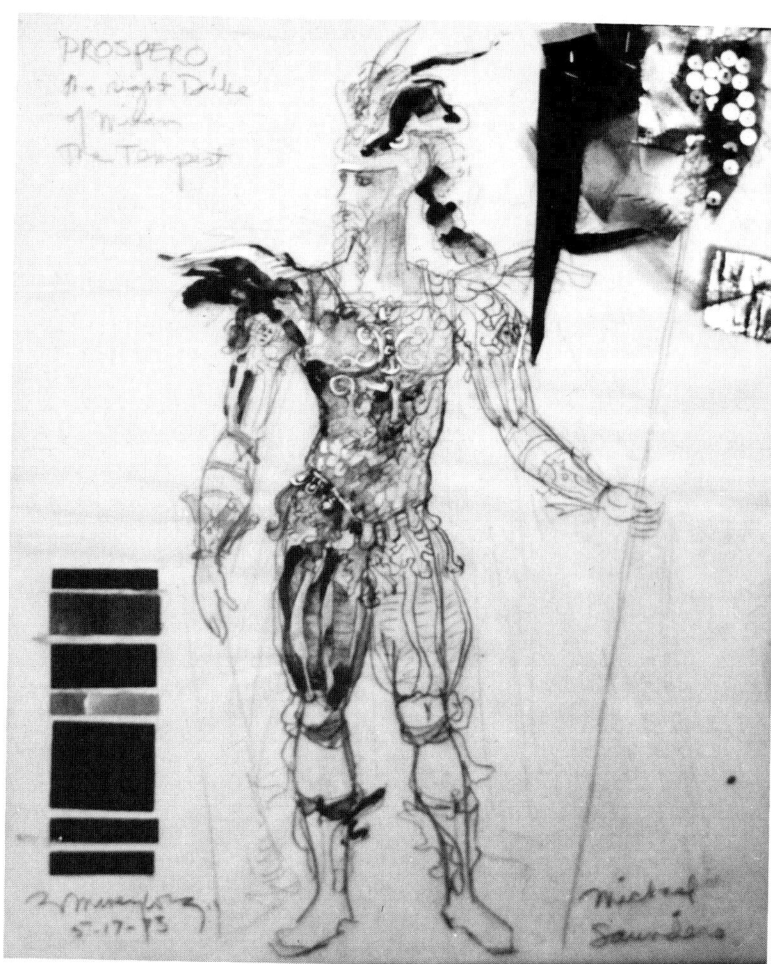

THE TEMPEST
Ballet, music by Tchaikowsky and choreography by Duncan Noble
North Carolina Dance Theatre, 1974
left Iris *right* Prospero

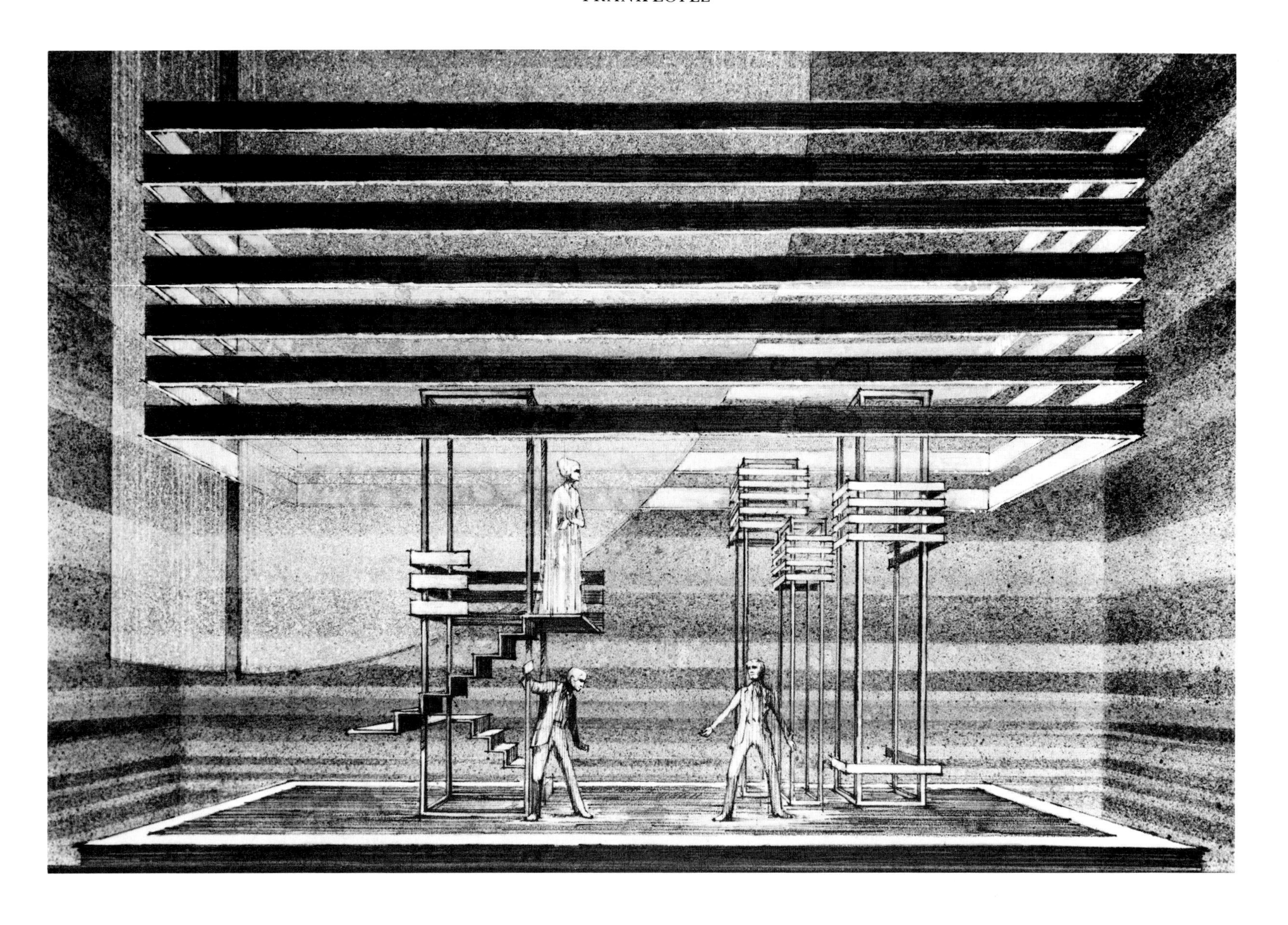

THE VISIT
by Friedrich Dürrenmatt, Project, 1974
Act II

WIPE-OUT GAMES
by Eugène Ionesco
Arena Stage, Washington, D.C., 1971
Model of set design

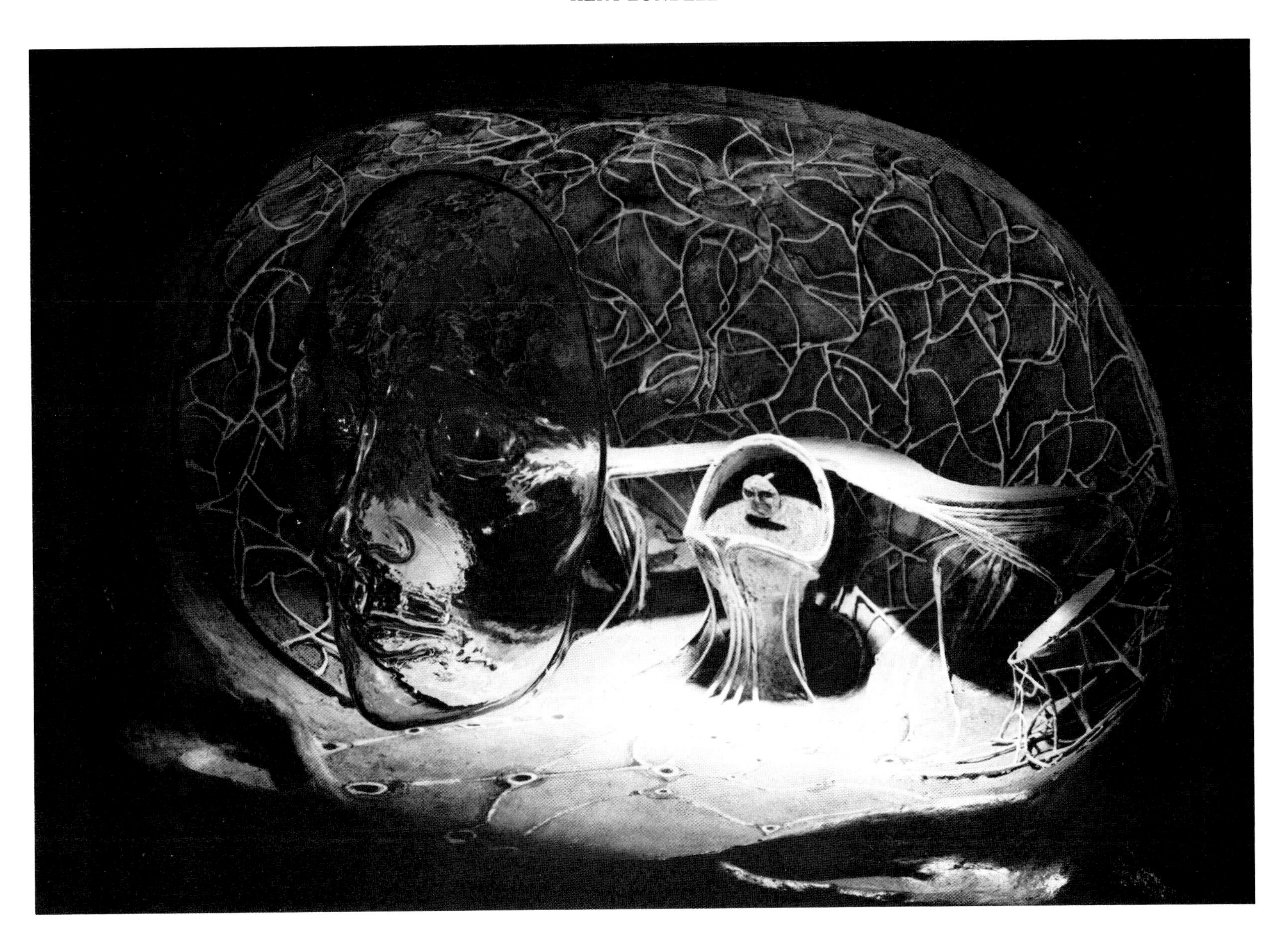

BRAIN CHILD
by Maxine Klein
Forrest Theatre, Philadelphia, Pennsylvania, 1974
Model of set design

DEAR OSCAR
by Young and Fieger
Playhouse Theatre, New York City, 1972
left Lady Mount-Temple *right* Oscar Wilde

THE THREEPENNY OPERA
by Brecht and Weill
Goodman Theatre, Chicago, Illinois, 1970

PEER GYNT
by Henrik Ibsen
Zellerbach Playhouse, University of California, Berkeley, California, 1972
Unit setting

RAISIN
by Hansberry, Nemiroff, Zaltzberg, Woldin and Brittan
Forty-sixth Street Theatre, New York City, 1973
Model of set design

SANDRA KATHLEEN FINNEY

GORDON JULES MICUNIS

THE THREEPENNY OPERA
by Brecht and Weill
University of Hawaii, Honolulu, Hawaii, 1973
left The Gang *right* Jenny Diver

THE VENETIAN TWINS
by Carlo Goldoni
Guthrie Theatre, Minneapolis, Minnesota, 1970
Columbina

THE VENETIAN TWINS
by Carlo Goldoni
Guthrie Theatre, Minneapolis, Minnesota, 1970

1776
by Stone and Edwards
Forty-sixth Street Theatre, New York City, 1969
The Congress: morning scene

A FLEA IN HER EAR
by Georges Feydeau
Repertory Theatre, St. Louis, Missouri, 1973
Olympe

SHORT EYES
by Miguel Piñero
Beaumont Theatre, New York City, 1974
Model of set design

NEIL DIAMOND: ONE MAN SHOW
Winter Garden, New York City, 1972
Model of set design

DON CARLO
by Giuseppe Verdi
San Antonio, Texas, 1968
Philip's study

DIE FRAU OHNE SCHATTEN
by Richard Strauss
Metropolitan Opera, New York City, 1966
Act I, Scene 1

HUNGER AND THIRST
by Eugène Ionesco
Berkshire Theatre Festival, Stockbridge, Massachusetts, 1969
Wall of history (bas relief)

THE LIFE AND TIMES OF JOSEPH STALIN
by Robert Wilson
Brooklyn Academy of Music, Brooklyn, New York, 1973
Bedroom

THE NIGHT OF THE IGUANA
by Tennessee Williams
University of Southern California, Los Angeles, California, 1973
Model of set design

THE WALTZ OF THE TOREADORS
by Jean Anouilh
University of Southern California, Los Angeles, California, 1972
left Mme. Dupont-Fredaine *right* Estelle and Sidonia

THE HOT L BALTIMORE
by Lanford Wilson
Center Stage, Baltimore, Maryland, 1973

THE MERRY WIVES OF WINDSOR
by William Shakespeare
Delacorte Theatre, New York City, 1974
left Falstaff as Aunt of Brentford *right* Mrs. Page

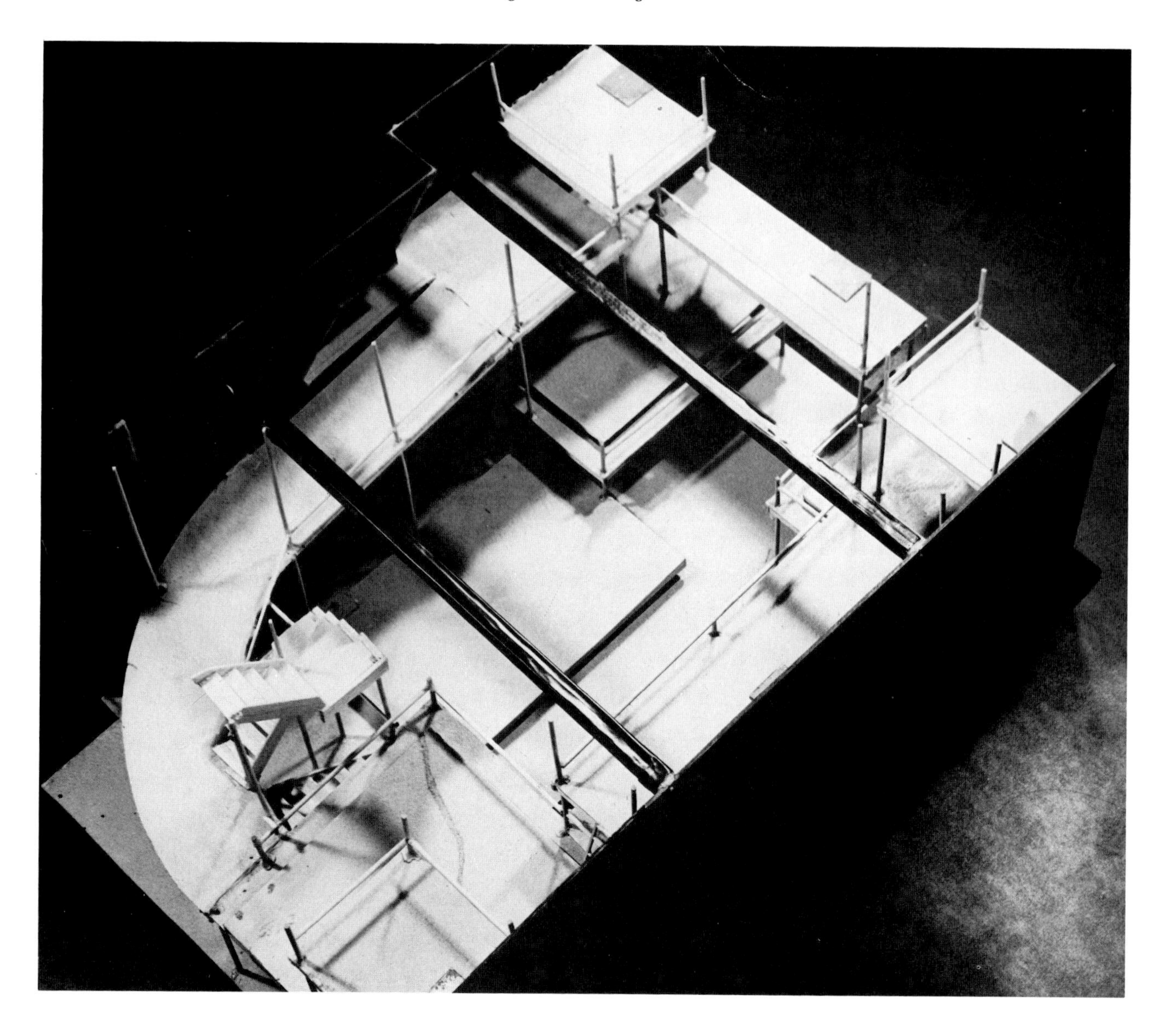

MAKBETH
devised by Richard Schechner from Shakespeare's play
Performance Group, New York City, 1970
Model of environment

PINKVILLE
by George Tabori
American Place Theatre, New York City, 1971

THE SAINT OF BLEECKER STREET
by Gian Carlo Menotti
Baltimore Opera Company, Baltimore, Maryland, 1973
Act I, Scene 2

THE EDUCATION OF H*Y*M*A*N K*A*P*L*A*N
by Zavin, Nassau and Brand
Alvin Theatre, New York City, 1968
Street

THE KARL MARX PLAY
by Rochelle Owens
American Place Theatre, New York City, 1973
Scene 1

SAINT JOAN OF THE STOCKYARDS
by Bertolt Brecht
Annenberg Center, University of Pennsylvania, Philadelphia, Pennsylvania, 1971
left Joan (Act II) *right* Small Speculators

FOLLIES
by Sondheim and Goldman
Winter Garden, New York City, 1971
Model of set design with lace insert

MACBETH
by William Shakespeare
American Shakespeare Festival, Stratford, Connecticut, 1973
left Sleepwalking scene *right* Heath

HORATIO
by Ron Whyte
Repertory Theatre, St. Louis, Missouri, 1971
left Claremont *right* Elsie

INDIANS
by Arthur Kopit
Brooks Atkinson Theatre, New York City, 1969
Model of set design

THE RISE AND FALL OF THE CITY OF MAHAGONNY
by Brecht and Weill
Yale Repertory Theatre, New Haven, Connecticut, 1974
Act II, Scene 13

ROSS
by Terence Rattigan, Project, 1973
left Lawrence (Scene 18) *right* Auda's Guard

AH, WILDERNESS!
by Eugene O'Neill, Project, 1969
left Belle (Act II) *right* Muriel (Act III)

THE BEGGAR'S OPERA
by John Gay
Chelsea Theatre Center, Brooklyn, New York, 1972

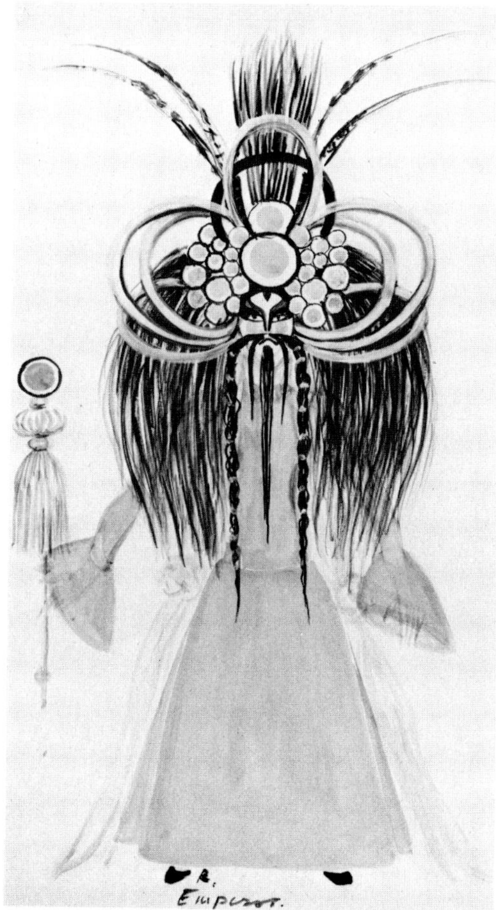

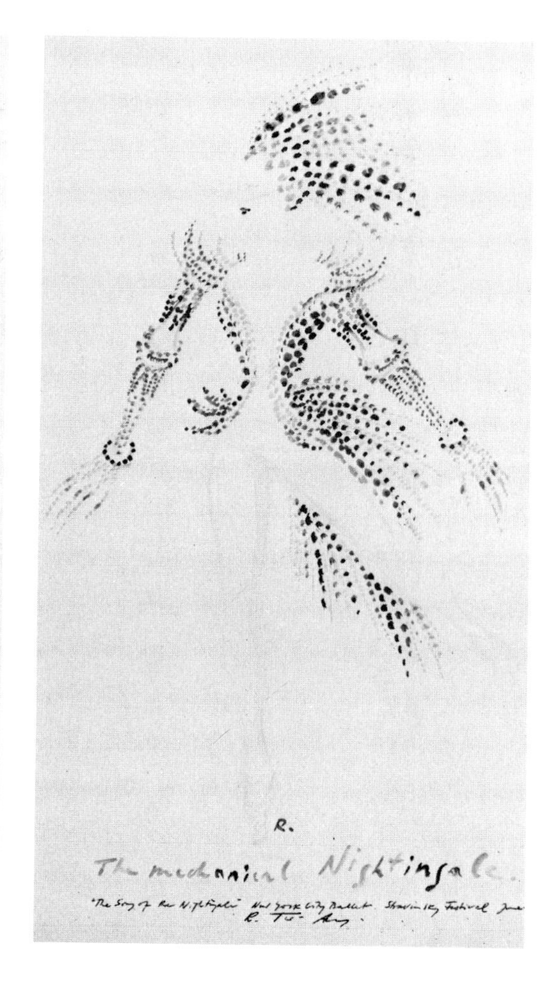

THE SONG OF THE NIGHTINGALE
Ballet, music by Igor Stravinsky and choreography by John Taras
New York City Ballet, 1972
left Nightingale *center* Emperor *right* Mechanical Nightingale

ALL OVER
by Edward Albee
Martin Beck Theatre, New York City, 1971

CYRANO DE BERGERAC
by Edmond Rostand
Zellerbach Playhouse, University of California, Berkeley, California, 1971
left Flower Girl *right* Orange Girl

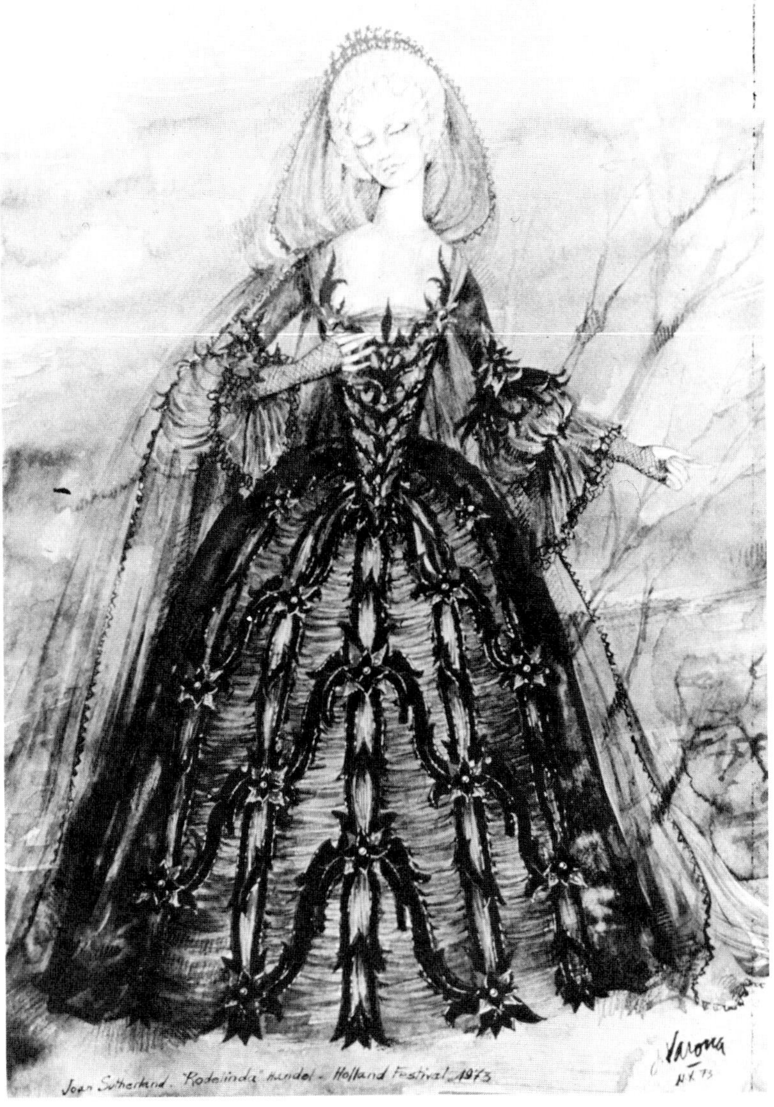

RODELINDA
by George Frederick Handel
Holland Festival, 1973
Costumes for Rodelinda

THE GOOD DOCTOR
by Neil Simon
Eugene O'Neill Theatre, New York City, 1973
left General Brassilhov *center* Mme. Cherdsakov *right* Peter Semyonich

PIPPIN
by Schwartz and Hirson
Imperial Theatre, New York City, 1972

THE ICEMAN COMETH
by Eugene O'Neill
Long Wharf Theatre, New Haven, Connecticut, 1972
Model of set design

LES TROYENS
by Hector Berlioz
Metropolitan Opera, New York City, 1974
Model of set design (two arrangements)

THE AMEN CORNER
by James Baldwin
Theater an der Wein, Vienna, Austria, 1965
Act II

THE AMEN CORNER
by James Baldwin
Theater an der Wein, Vienna, Austria, 1965
Act I

OUT CRY
by Tennessee Williams
Lyceum Theatre, New York City, 1973
Opening: Backstage

MACBETH
Opera by Ernest Bloch
Juilliard School American Opera Center, New York City, 1973

WAITING FOR GODOT
by Samuel Beckett
Guthrie Theatre, Minneapolis, Minnesota, 1973
Pozzo

1776
by Stone and Edwards
Forty-sixth Street Theatre, New York City, 1969
Drummer Boy

CATALOGUE OF THE EXHIBITION

Contemporary Stage Design—U.S.A. opened at the Library and Museum of the Performing Arts, Lincoln Center, New York City, on December 16, 1974.
**Works illustrated are preceded by an asterisk.*

Boris Aronson

Company, book by George Furth, music and lyrics by Stephen Sondheim, produced and directed by Harold Prince, Alvin Theatre, New York City, 1970. *Model of set design.*

Fidelio, opera by Ludwig van Beethoven, directed by Otto Schenk, Metropolitan Opera, New York City, 1970. *Set designs: Dungeon, Courtyard of Prison.*

Follies, book by James Goldman, music and lyrics by Stephen Sondheim, directed by Harold Prince and Michael Bennett, produced by Harold Prince, Winter Garden, New York City, 1971. **Model of set design; *collage of lace insert; preliminary rendering.*

Mabel Astarloa

Children of Faith, dance, music by Paul Hindemith, choreography by Renate Schottelius, Boston Dance Theatre of the Boston Conservatory of Music, Boston, Massachusetts, 1973. *Costume designs: *Sukey (Pas de Deux), *Roy (Pas de Deux), Big D, Red Girl.*

Howard Bay

Cry for Us All, book by William Alfred and Albert Marre, music by Mitch Leigh, lyrics by William Alfred and Phyllis Robinson, directed by Albert Marre, produced by Mitch Leigh, Broadhurst Theatre, New York City, 1970. *Set design.*

Halloween, book and lyrics by Sidney Michaels, music by Mitch Leigh, directed by Albert Marre, produced by Albert W. Selden and Jerome Minskoff, Florida State University Theatre, Tallahassee, Florida, 1972. *Projection designs: *Haunted House, Barbershop, Arctic, Cove.*

Man of La Mancha, book by Dale Wasserman, music by Mitch Leigh, lyrics by Joe Darion, directed by Albert Marre, produced by Albert W. Selden and Hal James, ANTA Washington Square Theatre, New York City, 1965. **Set design.*

Odyssey, book and lyrics by Erich Segal, music by Mitch Leigh, directed by Albert Marre, produced by Roger L. Stevens, John F. Kennedy Center for the Performing Arts, Washington, D.C., 1974. *Model of set design.*

John Lee Beatty

The Way of the World by William Congreve, Project, 1972. *Set designs: Act II; *Act III.*

Warner Blake

Brain, conceived and directed by Maxine Klein, Boston University Theatre, Boston, Massachusetts, 1972. **Rendering of set and environment as viewed from rear of orchestra level.*

Zack L. Brown

Lulu, opera by Alban Berg, Project, 1973. *Costume designs: *Animal Tamer (Prologue), *Lulu (Prologue), Lulu (I-1), *Schigolch (I-2), Countess Geschwitz, Lulu (II-1).*

Jeanne Button

Henry V by William Shakespeare, directed by Michael Kahn, American Shakespeare Festival, Stratford, Connecticut, 1969. *Costume designs: *Constable of France, *King of France.*

The Rise and Fall of the City of Mahagonny by Bertolt Brecht and Kurt Weill, directed by Alvin Epstein, Yale Repertory Theatre, New Haven, Connecticut, 1974. *Costume designs: Chorus Girl 1, Chorus Girl 2, Chorus Girl 3, Widow Begbick.*

Patton Campbell

The Makropoulos Affair, opera by Leoš Janáček after the play by Karel Capek, directed by Frank Corsaro, New York City Opera, New York State Theatre, New York City, 1970. *Costume designs: *Emilia Marty (I), *Emilia Marty (III) courtesy collection of John White, *Elina Makropoulos (Prologue).*

John Conklin

The Hostage by Brendan Behan, directed by Norman Gevanthor, Arena Stage, Kreeger Theatre, Washington, D.C., 1972. **Model of set design.*

Karen R. Connolly

The Lower Depths by Maxim Gorky, Project, 1973. **Costume and set design.*

Laura Crow

Warp by Bury St. Edmund and Stuart Gordon, directed by Stuart Gordon, produced by Anthony D'Amato and the Organic Theatre Company, Ambassador Theatre, New York City, 1973. *Costume designs: *Valaria, Insect Sorceress (I); *Chaos, Prince of Madness (II).*

Marianne Custer

Tosca, opera by Giacomo Puccini, directed by Edward Amor, University of Wisconsin, Madison, Wisconsin, 1972. *Costume designs: *Tosca (II), *Scarpia (I).*

Robert Edward Darling

The Visit of the Old Lady, opera by Gottfried von Einem after the play by Friedrich Dürrenmatt, directed by Francis Ford Coppola, San Francisco Opera, War Memorial Opera House, San Francisco, California, 1972. *Set designs: Town Hall, *Railroad Station. Costume design: Claire Zachanassian.*

The White Liars by Peter Shaffer, directed by Maurice Breslow, Long Wharf Theatre, New Haven, Connecticut, 1970. *Set design.*

JOHN DÖEPP

I, Said the Fly by June Havoc, directed by Eric Christmas, Guthrie Theatre, Minneapolis, Minnesota, 1973. *Set design.*

Treemonisha, opera by Scott Joplin, directed by Katherine Dunham, Wolf Trap Farm Park for the Performing Arts, Vienna, Virginia, 1972. *Costume designs: *Treemonisha, *Zodzetrick.*

Troilus and Cressida by William Shakespeare, directed by Ellie Chamberlain, Shakespeare Summer Festival, Sylvan Theatre, Washington, D.C., 1972. *Set designs: Study for Stage Left Tower, Study for Stage Right Tower, *Death of Hector (courtesy collection of Mrs. C. L. Reed).*

WILLIAM AND JEAN ECKART

*The Education of H*Y*M*A*N K*A*P*L*A*N,* book by Benjamin Bernard Zavin, music and lyrics by Paul Nassau and Oscar Brand, directed by George Abbott, produced by André Goulston and Jack Farren, Alvin Theatre, New York City, 1968. *Set designs: Ellis Island, Courtroom, *Street, Kaplan's Room.*

Mame, book by Jerome Lawrence and Robert E. Lee, music and lyrics by Jerry Herman, directed by Gene Saks, produced by Fryer, Carr and Harris, Winter Garden, New York City, 1966. *Set designs: *Literary Period, Open a New Window.*

KARL EIGSTI

The Karl Marx Play by Rochelle Owens, directed by Mel Shapiro, American Place Theatre, New York City, 1973. *Set designs: *Scene 1; *Finale.*

Serjeant Musgrave's Dance by John Arden, directed by Mel Shapiro, Guthrie Theatre, Minneapolis, Minnesota, 1968. *Set design.*

ELDON ELDER

Amazing Grace by Studs Terkel, directed by Marcella Cisney, University of Michigan Professional Theatre Program, Mendelssohn Theatre, Ann Arbor, Michigan, 1967. **Set design.*

A Family and a Fortune, adapted from Ivy Compton-Burnett's novel by Julian Mitchell, directed by Duncan Ross, Seattle Repertory Theatre, Seattle, Washington, 1974. *Model of set design.*

Pantagleize, opera by Robert Starer after the play by Michel de Ghelderode, directed by Wilson Lehr, Brooklyn College Opera Theatre, Brooklyn, New York, 1973. *Set designs: Café, *Promenade, Rachel's Room, State Bank.*

JEFFREY A. FIALA

Don Carlo, opera by Giuseppe Verdi, Project, 1970. *Set design: Act II, Scene 2.*

Rosmersholm by Henrik Ibsen, directed by James Sweeney, University of Massachusetts, Amherst, Massachusetts, 1974. **Set design.*

SANDRA KATHLEEN FINNEY

The Threepenny Opera by Bertolt Brecht and Kurt Weill, directed by Glenn Cannon, Kennedy Theatre, University of Hawaii, Honolulu, Hawaii, 1973. *Costume designs: Macheath, *Jenny Diver, *The Gang, *Tiger Brown.*

RALPH FUNICELLO

Candide, book by Lillian Hellman, lyrics by Richard Wilbur, John Latouche, and Dorothy Parker, music by Leonard Bernstein, Project, 1968. **Set design: Marketplace.*

Dear Antoine by Jean Anouilh, directed by Kent Paul, Loeb Drama Center, Harvard University, Cambridge, Massachusetts, 1973. *Model of set design.*

JUNE B. GAEKE

Macbeth by William Shakespeare, directed by M. James Young, University of Massachusetts, Amherst, Massachusetts, 1973. *Costume designs: *Ceremonial Robes Group 1 (Thanes), Ceremonial Robes Group 2 (Thanes), *Lady Macbeth, Queen's Ceremonial Robe, General's Warrior Robe (Macbeth).*

JOHN PETER HALFORD

Romeo and Juliet by William Shakespeare, directed by Philip Burton, Shakespeare Summer Festival, Sylvan Theatre, Washington, D.C., 1968. *Costume designs: *Paris (III), Capulet (III), Tybalt (II), *Mercutio (II).*

PETER HARVEY

The Boys in the Band by Mart Crowley, directed by Robert Moore, produced by Richard Barr and Charles Woodward, Theatre Four, New York City, 1968. *Set design (collage).*

DAVID JENKINS

The Changing Room by David Storey, directed by Michael Rudman, the Long Wharf Theatre production presented by Charles Bowden, Lee Reynolds and Isobel Robins, Morosco Theatre, New York City, 1973. **Model of set design.*

DON F. JENSEN

Bartók Piano Concerto Number 3, ballet, music by Béla Bartók, choreography by Ben Stevenson, Harkness Youth Dancers, Tour of Germany, 1970. *Set designs: Opening and Closing; *Pas de Deux.*

I Love Thee Freely by Benjamin Bernard Zavin, directed by Moni Yakim, produced by the Candlelight Company, Astor Place Theatre, New York City, 1973. *Set design. Costume designs: Elizabeth Barrett, Robert Browning.*

FLORENCE KLOTZ

Follies, book by James Goldman, music and lyrics by Stephen Sondheim, directed by Harold Prince and Michael Bennett, produced by Harold Prince, Winter Garden, New York City, 1971. *Costume designs (4 sketches).*

A Little Night Music, book by Hugh Wheeler, music and lyrics by Stephen Sondheim, produced and directed by Harold Prince, Shubert Theatre, New York City, 1973. **Costume designs (6 sketches).*

ILSE KRITZLER

Cabaret, book by Joe Masteroff, music by John

Kander, lyrics by Fred Ebb, directed by Martin Ross, Brunswick Music Theatre, Brunswick, Maine, 1971. **Set design: Kit Kat Klub.*

SANDRO LA FERLA

The Knack by Ann Jellicoe, directed by Keith Fowler, Virginia Museum Theatre, Richmond, Virginia, 1970. *Set design.*

The Ruling Class by Peter Barnes, directed by Patrick Henry, Goodman Theatre, Chicago, Illinois, 1972. **Set design.*

Sebastian, ballet, music by Gian Carlo Menotti, choreography by Vicente Nebrada, Harkness Ballet, Harkness Theatre, New York City, 1974. **Set design. Costume designs: Chorus Member, Sisters.*

MING CHO LEE

Boris Godunov, opera by Modest Moussorgsky, directed by August Everding, Metropolitan Opera, New York City, 1974. **Model of set design.*

Much Ado About Nothing by William Shakespeare, directed by A.J. Antoon, New York Shakespeare Festival, Delacorte Theatre, New York City, 1972. **Model of set design.*

Myth of a Voyage, dance, music by Alan Hovhaness, choreography by Martha Graham, Martha Graham Dance Company, Alvin Theatre, New York City, 1973. *Model of set design.*

SAMUEL LEVE

Arco-Iris by Murillo Neri, directed by Abraham Medina, Teatro Republica, Rio de Janeiro, Brazil, 1968. **Set design: Curtain.*

WILLIAM IVEY LONG

The Tempest, ballet, music by Peter Ilyich Tchaikowsky, choreography by Duncan Noble, North Carolina Dance Theatre, Roanoke Civic Center, Roanoke, Virginia, 1974. *Costume designs: *Iris, *Prospero, Stephano, Caliban.*

FRANK LOPEZ

The Visit by Friedrich Dürrenmatt, Project, 1974. **Set design: Act II.*

SANTO LOQUASTO

The Dance of Death by August Strindberg, directed by A.J. Antoon, New York Shakespeare Festival Lincoln Center, Vivian Beaumont Theatre, New York City, 1974. *Model of set design.*

Pericles, Prince of Tyre by William Shakespeare, directed by Edward Berkeley, New York Shakespeare Festival, Delacorte Theatre, New York City, 1974. *Model of set design.*

Wipe-Out Games by Eugène Ionesco, directed by Mel Shapiro, Arena Stage, Kreeger Theatre, Washington, D.C., 1971. **Model of set design.*

KERT LUNDELL

Brain Child, written and directed by Maxine Klein, produced by Adela Holzer, Forrest Theatre, Philadelphia, Pennsylvania, 1974. **Model of set design.*

MARY MCKINLEY

Dear Oscar, book and lyrics by Caryl Gabrielle Young, music by Addy O. Fieger, directed by John Allen, produced by Mary W. John, Playhouse Theatre, New York City, 1972. *Costume designs: *Lady Mount-Temple, *Oscar Wilde.*

JAMES E. MARONEK

Red Roses for Me by Sean O'Casey, directed by John O'Shaughnessy, Goodman Theatre, Chicago, Illinois, 1969. *Set design: Act III.*

The Threepenny Opera by Bertolt Brecht and Kurt Weill, directed by Douglas Seale, Goodman Theatre, Chicago, Illinois, 1970. **Set design.*

HENRY MAY

Peer Gynt by Henrik Ibsen, directed by William I. Oliver, Zellerbach Playhouse, University of California, Berkeley, California, 1972. *Set designs: *Unit Setting, Pine Forest, Palace of the Troll King, Asa's Death.*

GORDON JULES MICUNIS

The Venetian Twins by Carlo Goldoni, directed by Robert David MacDonald, Guthrie Theatre, Minneapolis, Minnesota, 1970. **Set design. Costume designs: Servant, *Columbina.*

JO MIELZINER

Out Cry by Tennessee Williams, directed by Peter Glenville, produced by David Merrick Arts Foundation and Kennedy Center Productions, Lyceum Theatre, New York City, 1973. *Set designs: *Opening (Backstage); Prison Scene; Finale (Sunflower Scene).*

1776, book by Peter Stone, music and lyrics by Sherman Edwards, directed by Peter Hunt, produced by Stuart Ostrow, Forty-sixth Street Theatre, New York City, 1969. **Set design: The Congress (Morning Scene).*

LAWRENCE MILLER

A Flea in Her Ear by Georges Feydeau, directed by Frederick Rolf, Repertory Theatre at Loretto-Hilton Center, St. Louis, Missouri, 1973. **Costume design: Olympe.*

DAVID MITCHELL

Short Eyes by Miguel Piñero, directed by Marvin Felix Camillo, New York Shakespeare Festival Lincoln Center, Vivian Beaumont Theatre, New York City, 1974. **Model of set design.*

JIM NEWTON

Neil Diamond: One Man Show, directed by Joe Gannon, produced by the Shubert Organization and Ken Fritz, Winter Garden, New York City, 1972. **Model of set design.*

DONALD OENSLAGER

Antigone by Jean Anouilh, directed by Jerome Kilty, American Shakespeare Festival, Stratford, Connecticut, 1967. **Set design (courtesy Harvard Theatre Collection).*

Don Carlo, opera by Giuseppe Verdi, directed by Tito Capobianco, produced by the San Antonio Symphony, Hemis Fair '68, San Antonio, Texas, 1968. *Set designs: *Philip's Study (courtesy collection of Robert Tobin); Garden (courtesy collection of Gerald Leahy); Monastery of St. Just (courtesy collection of Father Fred Tollini).*

ROBERT O'HEARN

Die Frau ohne Schatten, opera by Richard Strauss, directed by Nathaniel Merrill, Metropolitan Opera, New York City, 1966. *Set designs: *Act I, Scene 1; Act I, Scene 2; Act II, Scene 2.*

WILLIAM PITKIN

Comedy, book by Lawrence Carra, music and lyrics by Hugo Peretti, Luigi Creatore and George David Weiss, directed by Lawrence Carra, produced by Edgar Lansbury, Stuart Duncan and Joseph Beruh, Colonial Theatre, Boston, Massachusetts, 1972. *Set design.*

Hunger and Thirst by Eugène Ionesco, directed by Arthur Storch, Berkshire Theatre Festival, Berkshire Playhouse, Stockbridge, Massachusetts, 1969. **Set design (bas relief): Wall of History.*

LESTER POLAKOV

The Life and Times of Joseph Stalin, written and directed by Robert Wilson, presented by the Byrd Hoffman School of Byrds, Brooklyn Academy of Music, Brooklyn, New York, 1973. *Set designs: Prologue; *Bedroom.*

THOMAS F. RASMUSSEN

The Night of the Iguana by Tennessee Williams, directed by Clarke Gordon, University of Southern California, Los Angeles, California, 1973. **Model of set design.*

The Waltz of the Toreadors by Jean Anouilh, directed by Clarke Gordon, University of Southern California, Los Angeles, California, 1972. *Costume designs: Ghislaine, *Estelle and Sidonia, *Mme. Dupont-Fredaine.*

RAYMOND C. RECHT

The Hot L Baltimore by Lanford Wilson, directed by John Stix, Center Stage, Baltimore, Maryland, 1973. **Set design.*

CARRIE F. ROBBINS

The Beggar's Opera by John Gay, directed by Gene Lesser, Chelsea Theatre Center, Brooklyn Academy of Music, Brooklyn, New York, 1972. *Costume designs: Macheath, Lucy Lockit, Jenny Diver, Suky.*

Julius Caesar by William Shakespeare, directed by Edward Payson Call, Guthrie Theatre, Minneapolis, Minnesota, 1969. *Costume designs: Brutus, Lucius, *Lady Citizens, Portia, Antony, *Caesar, *Calpurnia, Male Citizens.*

The Merry Wives of Windsor by William Shakespeare, directed by David Margulies, New York Shakespeare Festival, Delacorte Theatre, New York City, 1974. *Costume designs: Falstaff, Black Moth and Owl Fairy, Mrs. Ford, Fairy Children, *Falstaff as Aunt of Brentford, *Mrs. Page.*

Over Here!, book by Will Holt, music and lyrics by Richard M. Sherman and Robert B. Sherman, directed by Tom Moore, produced by Kenneth Waissman and Maxine Fox, Shubert Theatre, New York City, 1974. *Costume designs: Lucky, Two Sisters and Mitzi, Band Leader, Canteen Aprons.*

JERRY N. ROJO

Makbeth, a collage derived from Shakespeare's play, devised and directed by Richard Schechner, produced by the Performance Group, Performing Garage, New York City, 1970. **Model of environment.*

WOLFGANG ROTH

Pinkville by George Tabori, directed by Martin Fried, American Place Theatre, New York City, 1971. **Design of environment.*

BEEB SALZER

The Saint of Bleecker Street, opera by Gian Carlo Menotti, directed by Frank Rizzo, Baltimore Opera Company, Lyric Theatre, Baltimore, Maryland, 1973. *Set designs: Act I, Scene 1; *Act I, Scene 2.*

DOUGLAS W. SCHMIDT

The Good Woman of Setzuan by Bertolt Brecht, directed by Robert Symonds, Repertory Theatre of Lincoln Center, Vivian Beaumont Theatre, New York City, 1970. *Model of set design.*

Macbeth by William Shakespeare, directed by Michael Kahn, American Shakespeare Festival, Stratford, Connecticut, 1973. *Set designs: *Sleepwalking Scene; Lady Macduff Scene; Parapet; *Heath.*

A Streetcar Named Desire by Tennessee Williams, directed by Ellis Rabb, Repertory Theatre of Lincoln Center, Vivian Beaumont Theatre, New York City, 1973. *Set design.*

SHADOW a.k.a. BRUCE HARROW

Gloria and Esperanza, written and directed by Julie Bovasso, Zellerbach Theatre, Annenberg Center, University of Pennsylvania, Philadelphia, Pennsylvania, 1973. *Costume designs: Sun and Moon Woman, Skull Woman, Sword Angel, Gloria (II).*

Horatio by Ron Whyte, directed by Charles Haid, Repertory Theatre at Loretto-Hilton Center, St. Louis, Missouri, 1971. *Costume designs: *Claremont, *Elsie, Siamese Twins, Gladys.*

Saint Joan of the Stockyards by Bertolt Brecht, directed by Dennis Rosa, Zellerbach Theatre, Annenberg Center, University of Pennsylvania, Philadelphia, Pennsylvania, 1971. *Costume designs: *Joan (II), Wholesalers, *Small Speculators, Newsboys.*

OLIVER SMITH

Gigi, book and lyrics by Alan Jay Lerner, music by Frederick Loewe, directed by Joseph Hardy, produced by Edwin Lester and Saint-Subber, Uris Theatre, New York City, 1973. *Set design: Paris Park.*

Indians by Arthur Kopit, directed by Gene Frankel, produced by Lyn Austin, Oliver Smith, Joel Schenker and Roger L. Stevens, Brooks Atkinson Theatre, New York City, 1969. **Model of set design.*

Kelly, book and lyrics by Eddie Lawrence, music by Moose Charlap, directed by Herbert Ross, produced by David Susskind and Daniel Melnick, Broadhurst Theatre, New York City, 1965. *Set design.*

Mass: a Theatre Piece for Singers, Players, and Dancers by Leonard Bernstein, staged by Gordon Davidson and Alvin Ailey, produced by Roger L. Stevens and Martin Feinstein, John F. Kennedy Center for the Performing Arts, Washington, D.C., 1971. *Set design.*

ANTHONY J. STRAIGES

The Rise and Fall of the City of Mahagonny by Bertolt Brecht and Kurt Weill, directed by Alvin Epstein, Yale Repertory Theatre, New Haven, Connecticut, 1974. *Set designs: Act I, Scene 9; *Act II, Scene 13.*

Ross by Terence Rattigan, Project, 1973. *Costume designs: *Lawrence (Scene 18), Rashid, *Auda's Guard, Feisal.*

Women Beware Women by Thomas Middleton, directed by Tom Haas, Yale University School of Drama, New Haven, Connecticut, 1973. *Model of set design.*

SHERRIE SUCHER

Ah, Wilderness! by Eugene O'Neill, Project, 1969. *Costume designs: *Belle (II), *Muriel (III), Nat Miller (III).*

ROBERT U. TAYLOR

The Beggar's Opera by John Gay, directed by Gene Lesser, Chelsea Theatre Center, Brooklyn Academy of Music, Brooklyn, New York, 1972. **Set design.*

Raisin, book by Lorraine Hansberry, Robert Nemiroff and Charlotte Zaltzberg, music by Judd Woldin, lyrics by Robert Brittan, directed by Donald McKayle, produced by Robert Nemiroff, Forty-sixth Street Theatre, New York City, 1973. **Model of set design.*

ROUBEN TER-ARUTUNIAN

All Over by Edward Albee, directed by John Gielgud, produced by Theatre 1971: Richard Barr, Charles Woodward and Edward Albee, Martin Beck Theatre, New York City, 1971. **Set design.*

The Song of the Nightingale, ballet, music by Igor Stravinsky, choreography by John Taras, New York City Ballet, New York State Theatre, New York City, 1972. *Costume designs: *Nightingale, *Emperor, *Mechanical Nightingale.*

JOHN WARREN TRAVIS

Cyrano de Bergerac by Edmond Rostand, directed by Douglas Johnson, Zellerbach Playhouse, University of California, Berkeley, California, 1971. *Costume designs: Cyrano, *Flower Girl, *Orange Girl, Comte de Guiche.*

JOSÉ VARONA

Attila, opera by Giuseppi Verdi, directed by Tito Capobianco, Deutsche Oper, Berlin, Germany, 1971. *Set designs: Act I, Scene 2; Act I, Scene 3.*

Fuga by José Varona, directed by Oswaldo Riofrancos, New York Shakespeare Festival, Other Stage, New York City, 1970. *Costume designs: The Investigating Committee, Hans Christian Andersen, Arkael, Friar Barbael.*

Rodelinda, opera by George Frederick Handel, directed by Tito Capobianco, Holland Festival, Circustheater, Scheveningen, Holland, 1973. **Model of set design: Act I, Scene 2. Costume designs: *Rodelinda (3 sketches), Grimoaldo.*

TONY WALTON

The Good Doctor by Neil Simon, directed by A. J. Antoon, produced by Emanuel Azenberg and Eugene V. Wolsk, Eugene O'Neill Theatre, New York City, 1973. *Model of set design. Costume designs: *General Brassilhov ("The Sneeze"), Mme. Brassilhov ("The Sneeze"),*Mme. Cherdsakov ("The Sneeze"), *Peter Semyonich ("The Seduction").*

Pippin, book by Roger O. Hirson, music and lyrics by Stephen Schwartz, directed by Bob Fosse, produced by Stuart Ostrow, Imperial Theatre, New York City, 1972. **Set designs (8 scenes).*

Uncle Vanya by Anton Chekhov, directed by Mike Nichols, produced by Circle in the Square, Inc., Circle in the Square Joseph E. Levine Theatre, New York City, 1973. *Model of set design. Costume designs: Serebryakov (III), Helena (IV), Marina, Astrov (II).*

ELMON WEBB and VIRGINIA DANCY

The Iceman Cometh by Eugene O'Neill, directed by Arvin Brown, Long Wharf Theatre, New Haven, Connecticut, 1972. **Model of set design.*

PETER WEXLER

Les Troyens, opera by Hector Berlioz, directed by Nathaniel Merrill, Metropolitan Opera, New York City, 1974. **Model of set design. Costume designs: Hecuba, Priam.*

ED WITTSTEIN

The Amen Corner by James Baldwin, directed by Lloyd Richards, Theater an der Wein, Vienna, Austria, 1965. *Set designs: *Act I; *Act II.*

Ulysses in Nighttown by James Joyce, dramatized by Marjorie Barkentin, directed by Burgess Meredith, produced by Alexander H. Cohen and Bernard Delfont, Winter Garden, New York City, 1974. *Set design.*

ROBERT YODICE

Macbeth, opera by Ernest Bloch, directed by John Houseman, produced by the Juilliard School American Opera Center, Juilliard Theatre, New York City, 1973. **Set design.*

PATRICIA ZIPPRODT

Pippin, book by Roger O. Hirson, music and lyrics by Stephen Schwartz, directed by Bob Fosse, produced by Stuart Ostrow, Imperial Theatre, New York City, 1972. *Costume designs: Strolling Player, Giselas, Charlemagne.*

Scratch by Archibald MacLeish, directed by Peter H. Hunt, produced by Stuart Ostrow, St. James Theatre, New York City, 1971. *Costume designs: Captain Kidd's Friend, Dewolf.*

1776, book by Peter Stone, music and lyrics by Sherman Edwards, directed by Peter Hunt, produced by Stuart Ostrow, Forty-sixth Street Theatre, New York City, 1969. *Costume designs: *Drummer Boy, Innkeeper, Ben Franklin in Nightdress, Richard Henry Lee.*

Waiting for Godot by Samuel Beckett, directed by Eugene Lion, Guthrie Theatre, Minneapolis, Minnesota, 1973. *Costume designs: *Pozzo, Estragon.*

BIOGRAPHIES

BORIS ARONSON

Born in Kiev, Russia; has been designing for theatre in United States since 1925; on Broadway designed settings and often costumes for numerous productions including *Three Men on a Horse, Awake and Sing, Paradise Lost, Cabin in the Sky, Cafe Crown, The Rose Tattoo, I Am a Camera, The Crucible, A View from the Bridge, The Diary of Anne Frank, J.B., Do Re Mi, Fiddler on the Roof, Cabaret, A Little Night Music* and *The Creation of the World and Other Business;* designs for dance include Ballet Theatre production of *The Great American Goof,* New York City Ballet production of *Ballade,* and *Tzaddik* for the Eliot Feld Ballet; has designed for the Metropolitan Opera, the Phoenix Theatre and the Royal Shakespeare Company; designed the interior and sanctuary for the Community Center Synagogue, Sands Point, New York, and the interior, wood sculpture and bronze mosaics for Temple Sinai, Washington, D.C.; has had more than ten one-man shows and been included in many group shows; won Tony Awards for *Cabaret* (1966), *Zorba* (1968), *Company* (1970) and *Follies* (1972), the Maharam Award for Set Design, *Cabaret,* and the American Theatre Wing Award for Stage Design (1950-51); awarded Guggenheim Fellowship (1950); authored *Marc Chagall* (1923) and *Modern Graphic Art* (1924), both written in Russian and published in Berlin; member United Scenic Artists, Local 829; recently designed sets for *Dreyfus in Rehearsal;* currently working on his memoirs, paintings and sculpture in addition to his designs for theatre.

MABEL ASTARLOA

Born in Buenos Aires, Argentina; studied at Escuela Superior de Bellas Artes "Ernesto de la Carcova," Buenos Aires, Ecole Supérieur National des Arts Décoratifs, Paris, Slade School of Fine Arts, London, and Brandeis University; studied ballet for 17 years; has performed as a dancer and designed sets and costumes in Argentina; her set design for *El cuento del Amor burlado,* Teatro Municipal General San Martín, Buenos Aires, was chosen by critics as best set for a ballet (1965); designed costumes for *Home Monster* at Brandeis University and La Mama (1969), the Hasty Pudding Theatricals' productions of *The Boy Who Cried Beowulf* (1970) and *Rhinestones in the Rough* (1971), and Boston Conservatory of Music production of *Children of Faith* (1972) which was later performed in Lisbon during the Third International Summer of Dance; member United Scenic Artists, Local 829.

HOWARD BAY

Born in Centralia, Washington; studied at Carnegie Institute of Technology; has designed 150 Broadway productions, received two Tony Awards, two Donaldson Awards, a Maharam Award, and won a *Variety* New York Drama Critics Poll; his credits include *Man of La Mancha, Toys in the Attic, The Music Man, The Little Foxes* (original production and Mike Nichols' revival), *The Desperate Hours, Carmen Jones, Up in Central Park, Come Back, Little Sheba, The Children's Hour;* directed Bobby Clark in *As the Girls Go,* as well as the American premieres of Mario Fratti's *The Cage,* John Arden's *Workhouse Donkey* and Strindberg's *There Are Crimes and Crimes;* production designer on several films including Balanchine's *Midsummer Night's Dream;* television art director for *The Pueblo* and many TV series such as Hallmark, Omnibus and Maugham Theatre; served as president of United Scenic Artists, Local 829; board member National Society of Interior Designers; Advisory Council member of International Theatre Institute; recipient of Guggenheim Fellowship; has taught at Yale, Carnegie-Mellon, Ohio, Purdue and Oregon Universities; wrote the book *Stage Design* published in 1974; his work was exhibited in a one-man show at Lincoln Center Astor Gallery and in a touring exhibit under the auspices of the American Theatre Association; currently holds the Alan King Chair in Theatre Arts at Brandeis University; recent work includes designs for new musical, *Odyssey.*

JOHN LEE BEATTY

Born in Palo Alto, California; studied at Brown University (B.A., 1970) and Yale University (M.F.A., 1973); created and toured with his puppet theatre for three years; assistant to Douglas W. Schmidt (1973-74); designed Off Broadway productions *Some People, Some Other People . . .* and *The Wager;* designed Off Off Broadway productions *Marouf* for Manhattan Theatre Club and *Diary of a Scoundrel* for Gene Frankel's Workshop; designed sets and costumes for Brecht's *Baal* at Yale Repertory Theatre; currently resident designer at the Queens Playhouse where he designed *Room Service, Come Back, Little Sheba, The Amorous Flea* and *An Inspector Calls;* member United Scenic Artists.

WARNER BLAKE

Born in Rolla, Missouri; studied at the University of Minnesota (B.A.) and Carnegie-Mellon University (M.F.A.); resident designer for a musical stock company in Minneapolis for two years; scenic designer at Great Lakes Shakespeare Festival, Ohio, for two seasons; currently assistant professor, School of Theatre Arts, Boston University.

ZACK L. BROWN

Born in Honolulu, Hawaii; studied at the University of Notre Dame (B.F.A.), currently enrolled in M.F.A. Design Program at Yale University; designed costumes for *Enrico IV, Candida, The Servant of Two Masters, The Little Foxes* and sets and costumes for *The Duchess of Malfi* and *Die Zauberflöte* at Notre Dame; designed sets for *The Royal Pardon* and *The Balcony* and costumes for *Major Barbara* at Yale; designed sets for Yale Repertory Theatre's *Watergate Classics*

(1973) and for *Enrico IV* at Loeb Drama Center, Harvard (1972); designed sets for *The Threepenny Opera* and *Misalliance* for the Harvard Summer School Repertory Theatre (1974); his costume designs for *The Duchess of Malfi* (1972) were awarded first prize in National Intercollegiate Scenic Design Competition sponsored by Southern Illinois University.

JEANNE BUTTON

Born in Columbus, Ohio; studied at the Carnegie Institute of Technology and Yale University; has designed costumes for numerous Off Broadway productions; her designs for *MacBird* earned her a Maharam Award; designed *People Are Living There* and *Suggs* for Lincoln Center Repertory, and the American Shakespeare Festival and Broadway productions of *Henry V;* costume designs for opera include the Amsterdam State Opera production of *Satyricon* and Washington Opera Society's *Rise and Fall of the City of Mahagonny;* has designed for Juilliard School Repertory Theatre, Negro Ensemble Company, Yale Repertory Theatre, New York Pro Musica; Broadway productions include *The Freaking Out of Stephanie Blake* and *The Watering Place*; has designed costumes for many stock companies including the Tanglewood Music Theatre, Williamstown Summer Theatre, Antioch Summer Theatre, Penn State Festival Theatre; has taught at Sarah Lawrence College and Hofstra University; lectured for the Connecticut Commission on the Arts; currently associate professor of costume design at Yale; is publishing a *History of Costumes* in slide form.

PATTON CAMPBELL

Born in Omaha, Nebraska; studied at Yale University (M.F.A.); on Broadway designed costumes for *Man of La Mancha, The Glass Menagerie* (25th-anniversary production), *A Hole in the Head, Fallen Angels, Twenty-seven Wagons Full of Cotton* and *Trouble in Tahiti;* Off Broadway designed costumes for *A Month in the Country;* among 15 productions designed for Juilliard Opera Theatre, Opera Company of Boston, Central City Opera, Santa Fe Opera and New York City Opera are *The Ballad of Baby Doe, La Traviata* and *The Makropoulos Affair;* designed costumes for Tokyo, London and Los Angeles productions of musical version of *Gone With the Wind;* has taught design at Barnard College, New York University, Columbia University and Brooklyn College.

JOHN CONKLIN

Born in Hartford, Connecticut; studied at Yale University (B.A., M.F.A.); designed Broadway productions of *Scratch* and *Lorelei;* received Tony nomination for set design, *The Au Pair Man,* New York Shakespeare Festival Lincoln Center; has designed for many resident theatres including Hartford Stage Company, Long Wharf Theatre, Center Theatre Group, Seattle Repertory Theatre, Arena Stage, San Diego Shakespeare Festival, Williamstown Summer Theatre and McCarter Theatre; designed *Beatrix Cenci* for New York City Opera and other productions for the San Francisco, Houston, Baltimore, Washington, and Minnesota Operas, as well as for the New York Pro Musica; designs for ballet include productions for the Royal Ballet, Joffrey Ballet and Pennsylvania Ballet; designed costumes for *Pericles,* New York Shakespeare Festival in Central Park (1974); recently designed sets for *Juno and the Paycock* at the Mark Taper Forum.

KAREN R. CONNOLLY

Born in Salem, Massachusetts; studied at the University of Massachusetts (B.A., 1969) and University of Wisconsin (M.F.A., 1974); designed costumes at University of Wisconsin for *The Heiress, Artists for the Revolution* (a new play from the O'Neill Theatre Center), and sets for *The Heiress, The School for Wives, A Flea in Her Ear;* supervisor of costume shop, University of Iowa Summer Repertory Theatre, and designer of sets and costumes for opera *Albert Herring* (1973); designed backdrop for Wisconsin Ballet (1973) and for ballet *Venuvian Variations* by Al Wilkes at University of Southern Illinois (1974); currently assistant to Grady Larkins on staff of Larkins Studios, St. Louis, Missouri.

LAURA CROW

Born in Hanover, New Hampshire; studied at Boston University (B.F.A., 1967), University of Wisconsin (M.F.A., 1969), and University of London; resident designer at University of Wisconsin and Western Illinois University; designed *Mass Ritual* and *Theatre Piece #2,* modern dance works choreographed by Anna Nassiff, Expression of Two Arts Theatre, New York City; as resident designer at Greenwich Theatre, London, for three years, designed the world premieres of *A Voyage Round My Father, Forget-Me-Not Lane* and *Servants and the Snow;* designed industrial shows in England for Rank-Xerox, Avis and Elida Gibbs; designed costumes for world premiere of *Do It,* Traverse Theatre, Edinburgh; founding member of the Low Moan Spectacular, which produced *El Grande de Coca-Cola;* designs for *Warp* earned her the Drama Desk Award for Most Promising Costume Designer (1973-74); designed costumes for *The Hot L Baltimore,* Center Stage, Baltimore; as resident designer of Organic Theatre, Chicago, designed costumes for two new plays, *Bloody Bess* and *Sexual Perversity in Chicago;* recently designed costumes for Academy Festival Theatre productions of *The Little Foxes* and *The Play's the Thing;* designed new church vestments for St. Mary of Nazareth, Chicago; returned to Europe in fall of 1974 to design costumes for two new productions.

MARIANNE CUSTER

Born in Minneapolis, Minnesota; studied at the University of Minnesota (B.A., 1970) and University of Wisconsin (M.F.A., 1973); taught costume construction and designed summer seasons at Southern Illinois University (1970-73); resident designer, University of Colorado (1973-74); resident designer, Colorado Shakespeare Festival (1974); currently costume designer at University of Tennessee.

ROBERT EDWARD DARLING

Born in Oakland, California; studied at State University of California, San Francisco (B.A.), Yale University (M.F.A.) and Bayreuth Festspiel Meisterklasse, Germany; formerly design assistant to Will Steven Armstrong and Ming Cho Lee; member United Scenic Artists, Local 829; has designed numerous productions including *The Latent Heterosexual* (American Conservatory Theatre), *Desire Under the Elms* (Theatre of the Living Arts), *Incident at Vichy* (Williamstown Theatre), *Black Comedy/White Liars* (Long Wharf), *Uncle Vanya* (Charles Street Playhouse), *The Visit* (Seattle Repertory Theatre), *Long Day's*

Journey into Night (Fred Miller Theatre) and William Ball's New York production of *Six Characters in Search of an Author;* has designed more than 30 opera productions including *The Visit of the Old Lady* (American premiere for the San Francisco Opera), *Un Ballo in Maschera* (Lyric Opera of Chicago), *Anna Bolena* (Santa Fe Opera), *Salome* (Vancouver Opera), *La Bohème* (Western Opera Theatre), *Medea* (world premiere for San Diego Opera), *The Crucible* (Anchorage Opera), *Colonel Jonathan* (world premiere for Denver Opera) and *The Flying Dutchman* (Lyric Theatre of Kansas City); has designed for the San Francisco Ballet and the Royal Winnipeg Ballet; guest lecturer in stage, costume and lighting design at Stanford University (1970-71); recent work includes designing *The Seagull* (Williamstown Theatre Festival), *Parsifal* (San Francisco Opera) and directing and designing *Faust* (Edmonton Opera) and *The Flying Dutchman* (Kentucky Opera Association).

JOHN DÖEPP

Born in Buffalo, New York; studied at Carnegie Institute of Technology (B.F.A.; M.F.A., 1963); member United Scenic Artists, Local 829; as scenic and lighting designer, Virginia Museum Theatre (1963-68), productions included *The King and I, Fanny, The Miracle Worker, The Odd Couple, The Cherry Orchard* and *The Subject Was Roses;* designed scenery and lighting for *Another Part of the Forest* at Pennsylvania State University; as associate designer to Jo Mielziner (1968-70), worked on Broadway productions of *1776, Georgy, Child's Play, Look to the Lilies;* assisted John Conklin on *Scratch;* since 1970 has designed scenery and lighting for more than 15 productions including *Fiddler on the Roof* (Brunswick Music Theatre), *Peter and the Wolf* (Pittsburgh Ballet), *The Justice Box* and *The Mother of Us All* (Off Broadway), *The King and I* (North Carolina School of the Arts), *Troilus and Cressida* (Shakespeare Summer Festival, Washington, D.C.) and *I, Said the Fly* (Guthrie Theatre); designed lighting for *The Pleasure of His Company* at the Kennedy Center, and lighting and costumes for *Treemonisha* at Wolf Trap Farm Park for the Performing Arts; has designed numerous industrial shows; was architectural assistant to Jo Mielziner on designs for theatres at University of Southern Illinois, University of Michigan, and Convent of the Sacred Heart.

WILLIAM and JEAN ECKART

Mr. Eckart—born in New Iberia, Louisiana; studied at Tulane University (B.S. in Architecture, 1942) and Yale University (M.F.A., 1949). Ms. Eckart—born in Chicago, Illinois; studied at Sophie Newcomb College (B.F.A. in Drama, 1943) and Yale University (M.F.A., 1949). Together designed more than 45 Broadway productions including *The Golden Apple,* for which they won the Donaldson Award for Best Scenery for a Musical (1953-54), and *Once Upon a Mattress, Fiorello!, Never Too Late, Flora, the Red Menace* and *Damn Yankees;* Off Broadway they designed the scenery for several productions at the Phoenix Theatre including *Oh Dad, Poor Dad;* designed numerous television programs; designed the costumes for the film version of *The Pajama Game;* production designers for the film *The Night They Raided Minsky's*; they have designed for ballet, opera and industry; members United Scenic Artists, Local 829; taught stage design at Circle in the Square Theatre School and a seminar in design for musical theatre at the Polakov Studio & Forum of Stage Design; Mr. Eckart is professor and head of design curriculum, Meadows School of the Arts, Southern Methodist University; Ms. Eckart is a candidate for Master of Social Work Degree at the University of Texas, Arlington.

KARL EIGSTI

Born in Goshen, Indiana; studied at Indiana University, American University (B.A.) and University of Bristol, England (M.A.); received Fulbright Grant to study in England; worked at Bristol Old Vic (1962-64); resident designer, Arena Stage (1964-65); resident designer, Guthrie Theatre (1969-70); has designed at Long Wharf, Theatre of the Living Arts, Studio Arena, Lincoln Center Forum; principal designer at American Shakespeare Festival (1969-70); guest designer at American Place Theatre (1973); on Broadway designed lighting for *Grease* and scenery for *Inquest;* Off Broadway designed *The House of Blue Leaves, Boesman and Lena* and *Nourish the Beast;* designer of industrial shows for Armstrong Cork Company (1971-74); recently designed *Death of a Salesman, Who's Afraid of Virginia Woolf?* and *The Front Page* for Arena Stage (1974-75 season).

ELDON ELDER

Born in Atchison, Kansas; studied at Emporia State (B.S.) and Yale University (M.F.A.); has designed settings and lighting for many Broadway productions including *The Affair, Legend of Lovers, Take a Giant Step, Shinbone Alley;* for New York Shakespeare Festival designed sets and costumes for *Othello, Julius Caesar, The Taming of the Shrew* and others; designed sets for *Henry IV, Part 1* and *Richard II,* American Shakespeare Festival; Off Broadway designed settings and lighting for *Drums Under the Windows, Morning Sun, The Child Buyer, A Whitman Portrait* and others; in London designed sets, costumes and lighting for *A Whitman Portrait, Hot Buttered Roll* and *The Investigation;* has designed for Center Stage, Queens Playhouse, San Francisco Opera, Santa Fe Opera, Juilliard School, Ypsilanti Greek Festival, Seattle Repertory Theatre, and 33 musicals, light operas and operas for the St. Louis Municipal Opera; designed settings and costumes for television productions of *Helen Hayes: Portrait of an Actress, My Heart's in the Highlands* and others; theatre consultant and designer for Delacorte Theatre (New York City), American Shakespeare Festival stage (Connecticut), Ypsilanti Greek Theatre (Michigan), Bininger Center for the Performing Arts (Florida Presbyterian College), Sidney Laurence Auditorium (Anchorage) and Theatre II (Seattle Repertory Theatre); recipient of Guggenheim Grant for study of classical theatres; most recent work includes scene design for Seattle Repertory Theatre production of *Hamlet* (1974-75 season); professor of stage design, Brooklyn College, City University of New York.

CHARLES ELSON

Born in Chicago, Illinois; studied at the Universities of Illinois and Chicago (Ph.B., 1932) and Yale University (M.F.A., 1935); has taught stage design and lighting at Yale and at the Universities of Iowa and Oklahoma; was professor (now Emeritus) at Hunter College (1948-1974) and producer/designer of its Theatre Workshop; has designed and lighted settings for plays, operas and ballets; Fulbright lecturer in India (1959-60); American editor, *Stage Design Throughout the World,* Volume 1 (1956) and Volume 2 (1964); lecturer on theatre, Third Asian Institute on the Arts, Seoul, Korea (1974).

JEFFREY A. FIALA

Born in Racine, Wisconsin; studied at University of Wisconsin (B.S., 1967, M.F.A., 1970); technical director and scene designer at various Wisconsin community theatres; journeyman scenic artist, St. Louis Municipal Opera; designed for Summer Repertory Season, Provincetown Playhouse (1973); since 1970, assistant professor and resident designer, University of Massachusetts; member United Scenic Artists, Local 350; recently designed sets for new translation of *Woyzeck* and a production of *The Cradle Will Rock*, University of Massachusetts.

SANDRA KATHLEEN FINNEY

Studied at San Francisco State College (B.A. in Art, 1967, M.A. in Drama, 1969); lecturer and senior technician, University of California, Riverside (1969-71); assistant professor/costumer, University of Hawaii (1971-present); designed and built costumes for Marin Shakespeare Festival, California, productions of *The Tempest, Henry V, The Taming of the Shrew* and others; at the University of California, Riverside, designed and built costumes for many productions including *The Madwoman of Chaillot* and *Guys and Dolls;* designed costumes for *The Fantasticks* and *A Christmas Carol,* Hawaii Performing Arts Company; at the University of Hawaii has designed and built costumes for more than 15 productions including *The Country Wife, A Streetcar Named Desire, A Midsummer Night's Dream* and *Desire Under the Elms.*

RALPH FUNICELLO

Born in New York City; studied at Boston University and New York University (B.F.A., 1970); assisted Wolfgang Roth on two productions in Berlin; assistant to Ming Cho Lee and Robin Wagner; designed American premiere of Anouilh's *Dear Antoine* for Loeb Drama Center, Harvard; designed Off Broadway production of *A Gun Play* and New York Shakespeare Festival Public Theatre production of *The Hunter* (1972); resident designer (1974 summer season), Pacific Conservatory of the Performing Arts, California; resident scenic designer, American Conservatory Theatre, San Francisco, since 1972; recent work includes designs for *The House of Blue Leaves, A Doll's House, That Championship Season, The Taming of the Shrew* and *The House of Bernarda Alba.*

JUNE B. GAEKE

Born in Cleveland, Ohio; studied at the University of Wisconsin (M.F.A., 1971); designed and taught at the Universities of Massachusetts and Nebraska and State University College at Buffalo; designed costumes for the Studio Arena Theatre, Buffalo, and the Provincetown Playhouse; assisted David Toser at the Goodspeed Opera House, East Haddam, Connecticut; recently designed costumes for new translation of *Woyzeck* produced at the University of Massachusetts.

JOHN PETER HALFORD

Born in Warrington, England; studied at College of Art, Liverpool; designed costumes for London theatre (1957-59); for Granada Television, Manchester, designed costumes for the Royal Ballet's *Cinderella;* since 1961 has designed costumes for nine productions at the Shakespeare Summer Festival, Washington, D.C., including *Twelfth Night, The Merry Wives of Windsor, The Taming of the Shrew, Much Ado About Nothing* and *The Tempest;* designed costumes, Opera Theatre of Northern Virginia (1961-64), for *Tosca, The Barber of Seville, The Marriage of Figaro, The Bartered Bride* and others; for the American Light Opera Company (1964-66) designed costumes for *Carnival, The Desert Song* and *My Fair Lady;* recently designed National Public Radio Graphics Design Exhibition, Mt. Vernon, Virginia.

PETER HARVEY

Born in Quirigua, Guatemala; studied at the University of Miami (B.A.); was design assistant to Rouben Ter-Arutunian, David Hays, Robert O'Hearn, Ed Wittstein, Oliver Messell, William and Jean Eckart, Eldon Elder and Esteban Francés; has designed scenery and costumes for numerous productions during last 15 years including *Noye's Fludde,* St. George's Episcopal Church, New York (1964), *The Sweet Enemy,* Actors Studio Theatre (1965), the Off Broadway *Dames at Sea* (1968), and the New York, London, Copenhagen, Hollywood and Boston productions of *The Boys in the Band* (1968-69); designed scenery and projections for Annenberg Center, Philadelphia, production of *Gloria and Esperanza* (1973); designed scenery for New York City Ballet; teaches theatre and costume design at Pratt Institute, Brooklyn.

DAVID JENKINS

Born in Hampton, Virginia; studied at Earlham College (B.A.) and Yale University (M.F.A.); has designed scenery for the Cincinnati Playhouse in the Park, Theatre of the Living Arts, Long Wharf, Trinity Square Repertory, Goodman Theatre, McCarter Theatre and Arena Stage; designed New York productions of *Room Service, The Changing Room* and *The Freedom of the City;* designed scenery for *Tommy* and *Trip,* Les Grands Ballets Canadiens; art director for NET-TV productions of *The Widowing of Mrs. Holroyd* and *The Seagull;* recently designed scenery for the musicals *Juno* and *Boccaccio.*

DON F. JENSEN

Born in Emporia, Kansas; studied at the University of Kansas (B.F.A.) and Columbia University; designed summer stock productions at Pocono Playhouse, Dayton Music Theatre, Toledo Zoo Theatre; designed scenery for Off Broadway productions of *Irish Plays, Guitar, Oh, Kay!, Anything Goes* and *Brother Gorski;* designed costumes for Off Broadway productions of *Cock-a-Doodle Dandy* and *Winkelberg;* designed scenery and costumes on Broadway for *The Sunday Man* and Off Broadway for *I Love Thee Freely* and the revival of *Jacques Brel;* for the Harkness Ballet designed scenery and costumes for *Bartók Piano Concerto #3* and *Shindig;* was assistant designer at Metropolitan Opera for *Die Frau ohne Schatten, Der Rosenkavalier, Hänsel und Gretel* and *Otello;* recently designed Off Broadway musical version of *Peg o' My Heart.*

FLORENCE KLOTZ

Born in New York City; studied at the Parsons School of Design; assistant to costume designer on original productions of *Flower Drum Song, Cat on a Hot Tin Roof, The Sound of Music, The Apple Tree, Golden Boy* and others; designed costumes for numerous Broadway productions including *Take Her, She's Mine, Never Too Late, The Owl and the Pussycat, Superman, Nobody Loves an Albatross,*

Follies and *A Little Night Music;* designed costumes for New York City Center revivals of *Oklahoma!, South Pacific, Carousel* and *Annie Get Your Gun;* Tony Award-winning costume designer for *A Little Night Music* and *Follies;* recent work includes costume designs for *Dreyfus in Rehearsal* on Broadway.

ILSE KRITZLER

Born in New York City; studied at Syracuse University, Pratt Institute and the Polakov Studio & Forum of Stage Design; designed numerous productions for the Cecilwood Theatre, Fishkill, New York, among them *Any Wednesday, You Can't Take It with You, Luv, On a Clear Day You Can See Forever* and *The Knack* (1967-68); assisted Robert O'Hearn on designs for Metropolitan Opera's *Der Rosenkavalier;* for the Aspen Music Festival designed *The Bear* and *The Country Doctor* (1968-69); for the Brunswick Music Theatre designed *Cabaret* and *The Merry Widow* (1970-71); has designed for the Classic Workshop Theatre, Bel Canto Opera and the American Theatre Company; assisted Clark Dunham on designs for *Born Yesterday, Volpone* and *The Country Wife,* Philadelphia Drama Guild; designed *Les Mamelles de Tirésias* for Manhattan Theatre Club (1974).

SANDRO LA FERLA

Born in Torino, Italy; studied at Academy of Fine Arts, Rome (Degree in Scene Design, 1965) and University of Oklahoma on a Fulbright (M.F.A., 1967); designed productions in Rome for Teatro Stabile dell'Auila, Teatro Quirino and for Teatro Stabile di Trieste; exhibited at Ninth and Tenth National Exhibitions of Scenic Design, Venice (1964 and 1965); resident scene designer and instructor of scene design, Goodman Theatre, Chicago (1970-73), where he designed *Twelfth Night, Marching Song* and *The Ruling Class;* designed six productions for Virginia Museum Theatre including *Arms and the Man, The Knack* and *Marat/Sade* (1969-70); designed *What the Butler Saw,* Academy Playhouse, Lake Forest, Illinois (1971); designed productions for the Arlington Park Theatre, Illinois, including *Private Lives, The Prisoner of Second Avenue* and *You Never Can Tell* (1973); designed sets and costumes for world premiere of Menotti's *Tamu Tamu,* Studebaker Theatre, Chicago (1973) and for XVII Festival of Two Worlds, Spoleto (1974); designed Harkness Ballet production of *Sebastian* (1973); designed sets and costumes for *Le Coq d'Or,* Teatro Verdi, Trieste (1974), *The Consul,* Bunka-Kaikan Theatre, Tokyo (1974) and *The Medium,* Yubinchokin Hall, Tokyo (1974).

SAMUEL LEVE

Born in Russia/Poland; studied at Cooper Union, Pratt Institute, Mechanics Institute and Yale University; in New York designed numerous productions for the Shuberts, George Abbott, Maurice Schwartz, Rodgers and Hammerstein, the Theatre Guild and the Metropolitan Opera; his designs have also appeared on stages in Canada, Brazil and Israel; has designed television specials and dramatic programs; taught scene design at City College of New York and Baylor University, Texas.

MING CHO LEE

Born in Shanghai, China; studied at Occidental College (B.A.) and U.C.L.A. School of Applied Arts; apprentice and assistant designer to Jo Mielziner and Boris Aronson; member United Scenic Artists, Local 829; member American Theatre Planning Board, Theatre Projects Committee of N.Y.C. Planning Commission, Advisory Council of International Theatre Institute and the Board of Directors of Technical Assistance Group Foundation; taught scene design at New York University (1968-70), has taught at Yale School of Drama since 1969; as principal set designer, New York Shakespeare Festival (1962-73), productions include *Ergo, Hair, Two Gentlemen of Verona, Much Ado About Nothing* and Sophocles' *Electra;* designed ten productions for New York City Opera including *Faust, Anna Bolena, Julius Caesar* and the American premiere of *Don Rodrigo;* other opera designs include *La Favorita* (San Francisco Opera), *Madama Butterfly* (Opera Company of Boston), *Ariodante* (Kennedy Center), *Madama Butterfly* (Metropolitan Opera National Company), *Bomarzo* (world premiere, Opera Society of Washington), *Lucia di Lammermoor* (Teatro Colón, Buenos Aires) and *Julius Caesar* (Hamburgische Staatsoper); as principal designer, Juilliard Opera Theatre/American Opera Center (1964-70), designed *Fidelio, La Bohème, The Rake's Progress* and others; for Broadway designed *Mother Courage and Her Children, Billy, Slapstick Tragedy, Two Gentlemen of Verona, Much Ado About Nothing* and others; designs for regional theatre include *Henry IV, Part 1* (Mark Taper Forum), *Inherit the Wind* and *Our Town* (Arena Stage Cultural Exchange Tour of U.S.S.R., 1973); designs for dance include *Myth of a Voyage* (Martha Graham), *Missa Brevis* (José Limon), *Don Juan* (San Francisco Ballet) and productions for Alvin Ailey, and for Gerald Arpino of the City Center Joffrey Ballet; won Maharam Award for *Electra* and *Ergo;* his designs have been exhibited in New York, Connecticut, Ohio and California; recent designs include *Boris Godunov* (Metropolitan Opera), *Whispers of Darkness* (National Ballet of Canada), and *The Seagull* for Andre Gregory.

WILLIAM IVEY LONG

Born in Manteo, North Carolina; currently studying design at Yale School of Drama in M.F.A. program; designed costumes and scenery for Yale Repertory productions of *Geography of a Horse Dreamer* and *An Evening with Dead Essex;* designed sets and costumes for Duncan Noble's ballet *The Tempest,* North Carolina Dance Theatre; designed costumes for European premiere of Leonard Bernstein's *Mass* in Vienna; member United Scenic Artists.

FRANK LOPEZ

Born in New York City; studied at Columbia University School of Dramatic Arts (B.F.A.) and Yale University; has designed *The Time of the Cuckoo, Two for the Seesaw, The Chalk Garden, Harvey, The Student Prince, Goodbye Charlie,* among others, for the Saratoga Springs Spa Theatre, Dayton Theatre Festival, Cincinnati Star Theatre and Falmouth Playhouse; assistant to the designer on Broadway production of *George M!* and the Metropolitan Opera *Der Freischütz;* has designed extensively for television including such programs as *The David Frost Show, That Was the Year That Was* and *Jack Paar Tonight;* recently designed for TV *The Guinness Book of World Records* and *The Dana Valery Show.*

SANTO LOQUASTO

Born in Wilkes-Barre, Pennsylvania; studied at

King's College, Wilkes-Barre (B.A.) and Yale University (M.F.A.); has designed for Arena Stage, Hartford Stage Company, Yale Repertory Theatre, Charles Playhouse, Williamstown Theatre, Long Wharf, San Francisco Spring Opera, Mark Taper Forum, Opera Society of Washington, and Chelsea Theatre Center; designed sets for Eliot Feld's ballet *Sephardic Song,* the New York Pro Musica's *La Dafne* and the Broadway production of *The Secret Affairs of Mildred Wild;* as principal designer for the New York Shakespeare Festival, designed sets for *Sticks and Bones, That Championship Season, Macbeth, King Lear, Dance of Death, Pericles* and *The Merry Wives of Windsor;* received Drama Desk Award for the Public Theatre and Broadway productions of *Sticks and Bones* and *That Championship Season;* his design for *What the Wine Sellers Buy* earned him a Tony nomination.

KERT LUNDELL

Born in Sweden; studied at the Goodman Theatre and Yale University; designed 14 productions for the American Place Theatre, including *Hogan's Goat, The Journey of the Fifth Horse, La Turista* and *The Kid;* served as consultant on the new theatre building for the American Place Theatre; designed Broadway productions of *The Investigation, Aint Supposed to Die a Natural Death* and *The Sunshine Boys;* designed *Indians* for Arena Stage, *Solitaire/Double Solitaire* for Long Wharf, and numerous productions throughout Europe and the U.S.; received Maharam Award, Drama Desk Award and Tony nomination for design of *Aint Supposed to Die a Natural Death;* currently project designer/theatre consultant for theatres at Walt Disney World and Disneyland, theatre consultant for new Kalamazoo College Theatre; working on projects in urban design and mass transit; writing and illustrating a children's book.

MARY MCKINLEY

Born in St. Louis, Missouri; studied at Smith College (B.A.), Art Students League, National Academy of Art, and the Polakov Studio & Forum of Stage Design; has designed costumes for the Fred Miller Theatre, Wisconsin, and Barter Theatre, Virginia; assistant designer on many New York productions including *Carnival, On a Clear Day You Can See Forever* and *Hello Dolly!;* was associate designer of World's Fair spectacular *To Broadway with Love;* has designed five New York productions including *Dear Oscar;* designed costumes for the Harkness Ballet, *Holiday on Ice* and night-club revues; head of ABC-TV costume department for five years and designed many *Wide World Specials;* has recently been concentrating on her paintings which were exhibited at the Tarlow Gallery in Westhampton, New York (1974).

JAMES E. MARONEK

Born in Milwaukee, Wisconsin; studied at the Art Institute of Chicago (M.F.A., 1959); resident designer at Goodman Theatre for 13 years; has designed sets for productions at Edgewater Beach Playhouse, Ravina Drama Festival, University of Chicago, Hull House, Lithuanian Opera Company, Cincinnati Opera Company, Tenthouse Musical Theatre, Academy Playhouse and University of South Florida; industrial presentation designer for Admiral, General Electric, Zenith and others; author of *Designer's Notebook* based on his European and Russian travels; currently resident designer at the First Chicago Center for which he designed a new musical, *Sheba;* contributing editor and critic for *Chicago Guide;* associate professor in scene design and history of theatre, Goodman School of Drama; president Local 350, United Scenic Artists.

HENRY MAY

Born in Havana, Cuba; studied at the University of Illinois (B.F.A., 1943) and Yale University; designed sets and costumes for New York productions of *Five Queens, Moby Dick* and for New England Conservatory of Music's *Dido and Aeneas;* designed New York Philharmonic *Promenades* (1963); designed sets for *Julius Caesar,* first production of New York Shakespeare Festival in Central Park; art director for *Omnibus* TV series (1952-61); scene designer for television series, *Studio One* and *I Remember Mama,* and for TV productions of *The Barretts of Wimpole Street, The Beggar's Opera* and *Riders to the Sea;* designs for dance include Agnes de Mille's *Rodeo, Three Virgins and the Devil, The Art of Ballet* and *The Art of the Choreographer,* John Butler's *Playing Cards* and José Limon's *The Moor's Pavane;* has designed opera productions for television, the University of California and San Francisco Opera; currently professor of scenography, Department of Dramatic Art, University of California, Berkeley, where he has designed sets and costumes for many productions since 1963; recently designed American Conservatory Theatre/Public Broadcasting System's *Cyrano de Bergerac,* Inverness Music Festival production of *The Consul,* and for the University of California *The Rehearsal, Richard II* and *The Country Wife.*

GORDON JULES MICUNIS

Born in Lynn, Massachusetts; studied at Tufts College (B.A.) and Yale University (M.A.); has designed for New York City Opera, Opera Society of Washington, Baltimore Opera, Pittsburgh Civic Light Opera, American Shakespeare Festival, New Orleans Repertory Theatre, Guthrie Theatre, Atlanta Arts Alliance, Charles Playhouse, and the Continental Theatre Company; Off Broadway productions include *Jo, The Good Soldier Schweik* and *Up Eden;* was professor of design at C.W. Post College and lecturer at Oberlin College Music Conservatory; interior design consultant to George Nelson Company; recently designed interior and lighting for a new MacDonald's restaurant in New York and a production of *Camelot* for Brunswick Music Theatre; member United Scenic Artists Executive Board; teaches theatre arts, costume and scenic design at Barnard College.

JO MIELZINER

Born in Paris, France; trained in the fine arts in Europe and the United States; over the last 50 years has been associated with 300 productions; served apprenticeship with Lee Simonson and Robert Edmond Jones; his first major production was *The Guardsman* for the Theatre Guild (1924); other productions designed are *Winterset, The Glass Menagerie, Death of a Salesman, Street Scene, Summer and Smoke, Guys and Dolls, A Streetcar Named Desire, The King and I, The Innocents, Gypsy* and *Can-Can;* recent productions include *The Prime of Miss Jean Brodie, 1776, Child's Play* and *Sugar;* has designed, or served as collaborating designer or consultant on many new theatres including the Vivian Beaumont and Forum Theatres at Lincoln Center, Mark Taper Forum and the ANTA Washington

Square Theatre; a pioneer in stage lighting, he was consultant to CBS-TV during early days of television; designed the setting and lighting for first meeting of the United Nations in San Francisco (1945); member Board of Directors, U.S. Institute for Theatre Technology; chairman, American Theatre Planning Board; author of *Designing for the Theatre* (1965) and *The Shapes of Our Theatre* (1970); won Tony Awards for design and lighting of *Child's Play,* Maharam Awards for *1776* and *Child's Play,* and Drama Desk Award for *Child's Play;* holds honorary degrees from Fordham University, University of Michigan, University of Utah, Otterbein College; received the Brandeis University Award (1963), the New England Theatre Conference Award (1957), the Academy Award for Color Art Direction of the film, *Picnic* (1955); his designs have been exhibited in one-man shows at the Lincoln Center Library and Museum of the Performing Arts, Brandeis University, Amherst College, Virginia Museum of Fine Arts, Toneelmuseum in Amsterdam; recent work includes the designs for *Miss Moffat* and *In Praise of Love.*

Lawrence Miller

Born in Yonkers, New York; studied at Carnegie-Mellon University (B.F.A., 1966, M.F.A., 1969); as faculty designer at College of William and Mary, designed sets, lights and costumes for *The Fantasticks, The Devil's Disciple, Twelfth Night, Hamlet, The Unknown Soldier and His Wife, Mandragola, Of Thee I Sing* and *Phaedra;* as set and lighting designer for the Wayside Theatre, designed *Plaza Suite, The School for Wives* and other productions; designed sets for *The Amorous Flea, Dark of the Moon* and *Summertree* for the Wedgewood Theatre; set and lighting designer for Pittsburgh Playhouse Children's Theatre; designer for Chautauqua Opera Association (summer 1972) and for St. Louis Municipal Opera Association (summer 1974); as resident designer for Repertory Theatre, Loretto-Hilton Center, designed sets for *The Mousetrap* and *Hail Scrawdyke!* and costumes for *Room Service, Twelfth Night, A Flea in Her Ear;* at Loretto-Hilton recently designed costumes for *The Imaginary Invalid, The Hot L Baltimore, Henry V* and *Irma La Douce.*

David Mitchell

Born in Honesdale, Pennsylvania; productions designed for the New York Shakespeare Festival include *Short Eyes, The Basic Training of Pavlo Hummel, Trelawny of the "Wells", Naked Hamlet, The Cherry Orchard, Volpone* and *Macbeth;* designed *Steambath* for Ivor David Balding at the Truck and Warehouse, *Colette* for Cheryl Crawford at the Ellen Stewart Theatre, *The Threepenny Opera* for the Charles Playhouse, and *The Cherry Orchard* for the Goodman Theatre; has designed many operas including *Mefistofele* for New York City Opera, *Aida* for Berlin Deutsche Oper, *Il Trovatore* for the Paris Opéra, and *Macbeth* for Washington Opera Society; recent activities include designs for *The Wager* at the Eastside Playhouse and New York Shakespeare Festival's revival of *In the Boom Boom Room* at the Anspacher Theatre.

Jim Newton

Born in Rockdale, Texas; studied at University of Texas (B.F.A.) and Yale University (M.F.A.); has designed for the New Haven Opera Society, Barter Theatre, Corning Summer Theatre, Northland Playhouse, Fresno University, Pacific Conservatory and for various companies in Los Angeles area; has designed tours for Neil Diamond, Alice Cooper, Elton John and Gregg Allman; assistant art director on many television programs including *The Smothers Brothers Comedy Hour, The Flip Wilson Show,* and *The Emmy Awards 1971;* art director for over 300 TV commercials and programs including *Barbra Streisand in Las Vegas;* member United Scenic Artists, Local 816, and Society of Television and Motion Picture Art Directors, Local 875; for television recently designed *High Rollers, Fred Astaire Salutes the Fox Musicals* and *Just for Laughs.*

Donald Oenslager

Born in Harrisburg, Pennsylvania; studied at Harvard University (B.A., 1923) with George Pierce Baker in his 47 Workshop; as recipient of Sachs Fine Arts Traveling Fellowship from Harvard, studied theatre design and production in Europe (1923-24); has taught at several universities, most prominently at Yale School of Drama where he was professor (now Emeritus) of scene design (1925-1970); designed first professional production, the ballet *Sooner or Later,* for Neighborhood Playhouse (1925); has designed more than 250 New York productions including *Jezebel, You Can't Take It with You, My Sister Eileen, Born Yesterday, Sabrina Fair, Janus, A Case of Libel, Good News, Anything Goes* and *I'd Rather Be Right;* designs for opera include *Tristan und Isolde* (Philadelphia Orchestra Association), *Le Pauvre Matelot* (Curtis Institute), *Salome, Otello* and *The Abduction from the Seraglio* (Metropolitan Opera), *The Ballad of Baby Doe, A Masked Ball* and *Don Pasquale* (Central City Opera Association), *The Ballad of Baby Doe, Tosca* and *Der Rosenkavalier* (New York City Opera), *Orfeo ed Euridice* (Vancouver International Festival), and *Don Carlo* (Hemis Fair '68); designed sets for *Antigone* at the American Shakespeare Festival; was consultant on design of several theatres including the Montreal Cultural Center, Philharmonic Hall and New York State Theatre at Lincoln Center, Spingold Theatre of Brandeis University, and the John F. Kennedy Center for the Performing Arts; edited *Notes on Scene Painting* (1952), wrote *Scenery, Then and Now* (1936), *The Theatre of Bali* (1941), "Settings by Robert Edmond Jones" in *The Theatre of Robert Edmond Jones* (1958), and the preface to the second edition of *Drawings for the Theatre* by Robert Edmond Jones (1970); has had more than ten one-man shows since 1936; holds honorary degrees from Colorado College and Hartwick College; honorary Phi Beta Kappa, Harvard University; received several State Department grants for travel to Latin America, Yugoslavia, Iceland, Ireland and Finland to lecture and consult on theatre; won Tony Award for set design, *A Majority of One* (1958-59); member United Scenic Artists, Local 829; recent work includes completion of his new book, *Stage Design—Four Centuries of Scenic Invention.*

Robert O'Hearn

Born in Elkhart, Indiana; studied at Indiana University (B.A., 1943) and Art Students League (1943-45); among his Broadway productions are *The Relapse, The Apple Cart* and *Child of Fortune;* designed ten productions for the Metropolitan Opera including *L'Elisir d'Amore, Die Meistersinger, Aida, Samson et Dalila, Die Frau ohne Schatten, Hänsel und Gretel* and *Parsifal;* for the American Shakespeare Festival designed *As You Like It, Macbeth, Troilus and Cressida;*

designed *Kiss Me Kate* for the Los Angeles Civic Light Opera, *La Sylphide* for American Ballet Theatre, *Porgy and Bess* for Vienna Volksoper, *La Traviata* for Santa Fe Opera, *Tallis Fantasia* for New York City Ballet, *Falstaff* and *Gianni Schicchi* for Central City Opera; member United Scenic Artists; recent work includes designs for Strasbourg Opera production of *Carmen*, Central City Opera production of *A Midsummer Night's Dream* and Metropolitan Opera production of *Le Nozze di Figaro.*

WILLIAM PITKIN

Studied at the Universities of Mexico, Texas and New Mexico, Southwestern University, Bard College (B.A.), in Paris at Ecole Paul Colin and with Christian Bérard; Broadway productions include *The Cave Dwellers, A Moon for the Misbegotten, The Potting Shed, Invitation to a March, Seidman and Son, The Beauty Part, The Chinese and Dr. Fish, Comedy;* designed *The Threepenny Opera, La Ronde, Dear Oscar* Off Broadway; has designed for the American Shakespeare Festival, Theatre Guild American Repertory Theatre, Syracuse Stage Company, National Shakespeare Company (including the portable structural stage used for bus-and-truck touring); designed *The Glass Menagerie* for State Department tour of Europe and South America, and *Your Own Thing* for Festival of Arts, Monaco, by invitation of Prince Rainier and Princess Grace (1973); has designed for New York City Opera and Opera Society of Washington; designed settings and costumes for American Ballet Theatre's *Coppélia,* more than ten productions for City Center Joffrey Ballet, and *Schubertiade* for San Francisco Ballet; other productions include *Born Yesterday* for Rome Theatre Guild, *Hunger and Thirst* and *Adaptation/Next* for Berkshire Theatre Festival; recently has been preparing designs for a new Broadway musical and for San Francisco Ballet's *Romeo and Juliet.*

LESTER POLAKOV

Born in Chicago, Illinois; studied painting at George Grosz Studio and stagecraft at Columbia University; Broadway productions include *The Member of the Wedding, Call Me Mister* and *Mrs. McThing;* designed *Purple Dust, The Empire Builders* and *The Life and Times of Joseph Stalin* Off Broadway; for the Opera Company of Boston designed *The Bartered Bride* and *The Beggar's Opera;* designed *Wuthering Heights, The Golem* and *Il Trovatore* for New York City Opera; designed Paris production of *The Skin of Our Teeth;* has designed many films, industrial shows, expositions and for stock companies and educational theatre; director, Polakov Studio & Forum of Stage Design, New York City.

THOMAS F. RASMUSSEN

Studied at Yale University (M.F.A.); during last 15 years has designed scenery and costumes for numerous stage productions and motion pictures; has designed many productions for the American Light Opera Company, Washington, D.C.; instructor and staff designer at American University and University of Connecticut; resident instructor of scenic design and production designer at University of Southern California for two years; assistant art director for Rowan and Martin's *Laugh-In* television program for three years, and for 1970 TV production of Academy Awards Presentations; as production designer at Theatre of the Stars, Atlanta, designed *My Fair Lady, The Pajama Game, The Music Man* and others; scenic designer for *Under Papa's Picture* Off Broadway; recently designed scenery for *Juliet Prowse Show* at the Desert Inn, Las Vegas.

RAYMOND C. RECHT

Born in Staten Island, New York; studied at Carnegie-Mellon University (B.F.A.) and Yale University (M.F.A.); as resident designer for Center Stage, Baltimore (1972-74), designed *Julius Caesar, The Hot L Baltimore, Uncle Vanya, Hay Fever, Happy Birthday, Wanda June* and others; for the Barter Theatre (1973-74) designed *The Imaginary Invalid, Candle-Light, The Torch Bearers, The Odd Couple* and world premiere of *Straitjacket;* designed American premiere of *Happy End* for Yale Repertory Theatre; resident lighting designer for New Haven Ballet Company and American Chamber Ballet Company; lighting and media designer for New Haven Black Ensemble Company; currently lecturer in design at Goucher College and designer of television commercials.

CARRIE F. ROBBINS

Born in Baltimore, Maryland; studied at Pennsylvania State University (B.A.) and Yale University (M.F.A.); has designed costumes on Broadway for *Over Here!, Grease, The Secret Affairs of Mildred Wild, Molly* and others; for the Lincoln Center Repertory Theatre designed costumes for *The Good Woman of Setzuan, An Enemy of the People, The Crucible* at the Beaumont, and *The Justice Box, The Inner Journey, The Year Boston Won the Pennant* at the Forum; designed *Sunset* and *The Beggar's Opera* for Chelsea Theatre Center; has designed for City Center Acting Company, NET-TV, CS Productions Cable Television, Guthrie Theatre, Shaw Festival, Inner City Repertory Theatre, Studio Arena Theatre, Buffalo Philharmonic, New York Shakespeare Festival in Central Park, and Circle in the Square; recipient of Drama Desk Awards in costume design for *Over Here!* and *Grease;* recent work includes clothes for Lee Grant in NET-TV "Theatre in America" production of *The Seagull,* and costumes for City Center Acting Company production of *The Taming of the Shrew;* faculty member, Design Department, New York University.

JERRY N. ROJO

Born in Alton, Illinois; studied at Lake Forest College (B.A., 1957) and Tulane University (M.F.A., 1960); instructor at University of Omaha (1960-61); associate professor, University of Connecticut, since 1961; specializes in scene design, architecture, consulting and directing for environmental theatre; designed the environments for *Endgame,* Manhattan Project (1973), *A Great Hoss Pistol* for Section Ten (1973), and *The Tooth of Crime* (1972), *Commune* (1971), *Makbeth* (1970), *Dionysus in 69,* all for the Performance Group; has designed more than 50 productions at the University of Connecticut where he also directed *Our House, a Work in Progress* and *Baal Games;* designed environmental theatres for Section Ten in New York City, University of Connecticut, Sarah Lawrence College, an open-space theatre for the College of White Plains, and the touring environmental stage for Phoenix Theatre; his studies in architectural design include a modular theatre system for the Brooklyn Academy of Music, an open-space theatre for The Space, a convertible environmental theatre for the Murray Louis Dance Company; he has served as architectural consultant for Cabaret Theatre at Westbeth, New York City, and for the Theatre Department, University of Delaware.

WOLFGANG ROTH

Born in Berlin, Germany; studied at the State Academy of the Arts, Berlin; served apprenticeship in theatre design and painting and later designed at Erwin Piscator's theatre and with Bertolt Brecht; designed at state theatres, opera houses and private theatres in Germany until 1933 when he worked as a stage designer and architect in Austria; in Zurich (1934), created sets for vaudeville and variety shows, designed plays, operas, operettas, and also played part of a musical clown in vaudeville and circus; in London (1938), designed Piscator's *War and Peace;* became U.S. citizen in 1945; Broadway productions include *Porgy and Bess, Twentieth Century, Yellow Jack, Bernardine, The Tower Beyond Tragedy;* Off Broadway productions include *Johnny Johnson, The Good Woman of Setzuan, The Typists* and *The Tiger, Brecht on Brecht;* has designed for the American Repertory Theatre, ANTA Experimental Theatre, Margaret Webster Touring Shakespeare Company, Boston Repertory Theatre, Theatre of the Living Arts and Berkshire Theatre Festival; opera designs include *Don Pasquale, Boris Godunov,* and *A Masked Ball* (Metropolitan Opera), *The School for Wives, The Threepenny Opera* and *Danton's Death* (New York City Opera), and more than 20 opera productions throughout the world; creator, designer and producer of *The Littlest Circus,* a dance pantomime touring the U.S. and Canada since 1957; master teacher of stage design, New York University; recently completed new production of *The Threepenny Opera* for resident theatre in Munich; currently working on several new productions in Germany and writing his autobiography; his work in U.S. theatre is being exhibited by Academy of Arts, Berlin, in a tour of Western Europe (1974-75).

BEEB SALZER

Born in Cincinnati, Ohio; studied at Yale College (B.A.) and Yale School of Drama (M.F.A.); has designed over 25 operas for the Baltimore Opera, Wolf Trap Foundation, Manhattan School of Music, Friends of French Opera; assisted George Jenkins on several Broadway productions, on films, on productions for Jones Beach Marine Theatre and World's Fair pavilions; designed lighting for *Promenade* concerts, Lincoln Center (1964); designed *Take Three* Off Broadway, and productions for Cincinnati Summer Playhouse, Barnard-Columbia Summer Theatre, Drew University, Open Space Theatre Company, Teatro de Ensayo, Chile; taught design at Long Island University, University of Panama, Queens College; currently teaches at Lehman College of the City University of New York and is designing *Twelfth Night* for Open Space Theatre.

DOUGLAS W. SCHMIDT

Born in Cincinnati, Ohio; studied at Boston University under Raymond Sovey and Horace Armistead; has designed over 100 productions for Broadway, regional theatres, stock companies, opera and ballet throughout the country; his designs have been mounted at the Guthrie Theatre, Arena Stage, Juilliard School, American Shakespeare Festival and New York Shakespeare Festival; has been principal designer for Cincinnati Playhouse in the Park, the Music Theatre Project at Tanglewood, the Repertory Theatre of Lincoln Center, and currently for the City Center Acting Company; designed Broadway productions of *The Country Girl, A Streetcar Named Desire* (revival), *Grease* and *Over Here!;* won Maharam Award in scene design for Lincoln Center Repertory's *Enemies* (1973), a production which he also designed for NET-TV; recently designed new productions for Broadway, New York City Opera and City Center Acting Company.

SHADOW a.k.a. BRUCE HARROW

Born in Lakeview, Oregon; studied at San Francisco State (B.A. in Art, M.A. in Theatre Design), McKnight Fellow, University of Minnesota; designed costumes for *A Light Fantastic,* City Center Joffrey Ballet (1968), for *Idomeneo,* Caramoor Opera Festival, Katonah, New York (1970); for *Saint Joan of the Stockyards* (1971) and *Gloria and Esperanza* (1973), Annenberg Center, Philadelphia; designed *Welcome to Andromeda* and *Variety Obit* Off Broadway; designed *Horatio* for the Repertory Theatre of Loretto-Hilton Center, St. Louis (1971) and for Arena Stage (1974).

OLIVER SMITH

Born in Waupawn, Wisconsin; studied at Pennsylvania State University (B.A.); co-director of American Ballet Theatre since 1946; on Broadway designed and co-produced *On the Town, Billion Dollar Baby, Gentlemen Prefer Blondes, No Exit, In the Summer House, Indians;* ballet designs include *Rodeo, Fancy Free, Interplay, Fall River Legend, Les Noces, Swan Lake, Giselle;* Broadway designs include *Brigadoon, High Button Shoes, Paint Your Wagon, My Fair Lady, The Sound of Music, West Side Story, Hello, Dolly!, Auntie Mame, Beckett, The Night of the Iguana, A Taste of Honey, Barefoot in the Park, Dylan;* for the Metropolitan Opera designed *La Traviata* and *Martha;* designed *Don Giovanni* and *Die Fledermaus* for the San Francisco Opera, and for the Opera Company of Boston, *Falstaff, Carmen* and the American premiere of *Moses and Aaron;* designed the Bernstein *Mass* for the opening of the Kennedy Center in Washington, D.C.; member of Kennedy Center Bicentennial Planning Committee; currently master teacher of scene design at New York University; working on designs for full-length production of *The Sleeping Beauty* for American Ballet Theatre.

ANTHONY J. STRAIGES

Born in Minersville, Pennsylvania; studied at Brooklyn College and Yale University; designed sets and costumes for American Puppet Theatre, Washington, D.C.; for the San Francisco Summer Opera designed sets for *La Bohème, Rigoletto* and *Man in the Moon;* at Brooklyn College designed sets for *Exit the King, Oh Dad, Poor Dad, Ariadne auf Naxos,* and costumes for *The Lower Depths* and *How Music Came to Earth;* designed sets for Yale Drama School production of *Women Beware Women;* for Yale Repertory Theatre designed sets for *The Rise and Fall of the City of Mahagonny* and costumes for *Shlemiel the First;* recently designed sets for *Tuona, Princess of Burgundia* at Adelphi University.

SHERRIE SUCHER

Born in Jerusalem, Israel; studied at Cooper Union, Parsons School of Design, New York

University and the Polakov Studio & Forum of Stage Design; member United Scenic Artists, Local 829; has designed productions at La Mama and costumes for the films *Lucky Luciano, My Brother* and *Godspell;* won Young New York Film Critics Award as best costume designer (1973) for *Godspell;* has designed for television and industry; free-lance stylist for several production companies and advertising agencies since 1968; buyer of fashions for New York boutique.

Robert U. Taylor

Born in Lexington, Virginia; studied at University of Pennsylvania (B.F.A.), Pennsylvania Academy of Fine Arts and Yale University (M.F.A.); has designed numerous university and regional theatre productions for Loeb Drama Center at Harvard, Cincinnati Playhouse in the Park, John Drew Theatre, Goodman Theatre, Arena Stage and McCarter Theatre; designed *The Bacchae* and *We Bombed in New Haven* for Yale Repertory Theatre; has designed both Broadway and Off Broadway productions including *Touch, Unlikely Heroes, Lady Day, Sisters of Mercy, Fashion* and *Raisin;* won the Maharam and Drama Desk Awards for his designs for Chelsea Theatre Center's *The Beggar's Opera;* has worked as a musician, painter, interior designer and architectural consultant for several new theatres; recently designed productions for the McCarter Theatre and Arena Stage.

Rouben Ter-Arutunian

Born in Tiflis, Russia; studied and taught art, art history, theatre, music, philosophy in Berlin, Vienna and Paris; came to United States in 1951; member United Scenic Artists, Local 829; has designed scenery and costumes for innumerable theatre, opera and ballet/dance productions throughout the United States and Europe; among his theatre designs are *New Girl in Town, Redhead, Arturo Ui, The Milk Train Doesn't Stop Here Anymore, Exit the King* for Broadway, and *Eh!* and *The Party on Greenwich Avenue* Off Broadway; for the American Shakespeare Festival designed scenery and costumes for *King John, Measure for Measure, Othello, Much Ado About Nothing;* designs for opera include *Bluebeard's Castle, Hansel and Gretel* and others (New York City Opera), *Pélléas and Mélisande* (Spoleto Festival), and *Madame Butterfly, The Bassarids* and *The Devils of Loudun* (Santa Fe Opera); has designed dance productions for New York City Ballet *(The Seven Deadly Sins, Swan Lake, Ballet Imperial, The Nutcracker, Dybbuk Variations* and others), for Harkness Ballet *(Firebird, After Eden, A Season in Hell),* for Ballet Rambert *(Ricercare, Pierrot Lunaire),* and for the Joffrey Ballet, San Francisco Ballet, Glen Tetley Company, American Ballet Theatre, Pennsylvania Ballet, Alvin Ailey Dance Company, Royal Ballet, Royal Swedish Ballet, Royal Danish Ballet and others; designed NBC-TV opera productions in 1950's including *The Abduction from the Seraglio, The Magic Flute* and *Maria Golovin,* and many other television productions; winner of Emmy Award, best art direction, NBC-TV-Hallmark production of *Twelfth Night;* winner of Outer Critics Circle Award, best scenic design, *Who Was That Lady I Saw You With?;* winner Tony Award, best costume design, *Redhead;* his designs have been exhibited in one-man shows in New York City and Santa Fe; recent work includes design of scenery and costumes for *Anatol* (Akademietheater, Vienna), *The Relativity of Icarus* (City Center Joffrey Ballet) and *Coppélia* (New York City Ballet).

John Warren Travis

Born in Texas; studied at University of Texas (B.F.A.) and Stanford University (M.F.A.); designed costumes for Off Broadway productions including *This Property Is Condemned* and *Another Part of the Forest;* designed *The Milk Train Doesn't Stop Here Anymore* for Actor's Workshop, San Francisco; for California Shakespeare Festival designed costumes for *Hamlet, The Comedy of Errors, A Midsummer Night's Dream* and others; designed sets and costumes for Stanford Repertory Theatre productions of *The Chairs, The Marriage Proposal, Cock-a-Doodle Dandy;* designed costumes for *King Lear* at San Francisco's Palace of Fine Arts and *First Time Out* for San Francisco Ballet; for Berkeley Repertory Theatre designed sets and costumes for *Scapin, The Alchemist, Love's Labour's Lost, Heartbreak House;* designed costumes for *The Blacks, The Dream Play, Cyrano de Bergerac, Narrow Road to the Deep North, Henry IV,* Giraudoux's *Electra,* and sets and costumes for *Danton's Death* and *The Bacchae* at the Zellerbach Playhouse, University of California; assistant professor in costume design, University of California, Berkeley; recently designed sets and costumes for Menotti's *The Consul* at the new Frank Lloyd Wright Theatre in Marin County, California.

José Varona

Born in Mendoza, Argentina; designed sets and costumes for opera, ballet, theatre, TV and films in Buenos Aires; for the Teatro Colón, Buenos Aires, designed sets and costumes for *The Rake's Progress, Il Trovatore, Macbeth, Un Ballo in Maschera,* among others; since his arrival in New York (early '60's), he has designed for the New York Shakespeare Festival Mobile Theatre, New York City Opera, American Opera Center, Washington Opera Society, Kennedy Center, Baltimore Opera, Caramoor Festival, Pennsylvania Ballet, American Shakespeare Festival and San Francisco Opera; designed costumes for more than ten New York City Opera productions including *Julius Caesar, Der Rosenkavalier, Faust, Roberto Devereux, Maria Stuarda, The Tales of Hoffmann,* and sets and costumes for *Carmen;* designed sets and costumes for *Lucrezia Borgia,* Vancouver Opera, and Australian Opera Company's *Tales of Hoffmann;* in Europe has designed for the Hamburgische Staatsoper, Deutsche Oper Berlin, Paris Opéra and the Holland Festival; recent work includes set and costume designs for full-length ballet *The Sleeping Beauty* at Paris Opéra; currently working on set and costume designs for Gluck's *Orfeo,* Holland Festival (1975).

Tony Walton

Born in Walton-on-Thames, England; studied at Radley College, City of Oxford School of Technology, Art & Commerce, and Slade School of Fine Arts, London; designed many New York productions including *A Funny Thing Happened on the Way to the Forum, Golden Boy, The Apple Tree, Pippin, Uncle Vanya, The Good Doctor;* productions designed in London include *The Ginger Man, Pieces of Eight, The Most Happy Fella, Caligula, The Travails of Sancho Panza;* designed Verdi's *Otello* for the Spoleto Festival (1965); for the San Francisco Ballet designed *Harp Concerto* and *Mother Blues;* designed the Sadler's Wells production of *The Love of Three Oranges* (1963); has designed for Benjamin Britten's English Opera Group; was co-producer of London productions of *The Ginger Man, New Cranks, A Funny*

Thing Happened on the Way to the Forum and *She Loves Me;* has designed several films including *Mary Poppins, A Funny Thing Happened on the Way to the Forum, The Boy Friend* and *Murder on the Orient Express;* designed American television production *Free to Be You and Me;* won Tony and Drama Desk Awards for his scenery for *Pippin;* is noted for his book illustrations; has had a number of one-man exhibitions in New York and London; recently designed sets for the forthcoming Broadway musical, *Chicago.*

Elmon Webb and Virginia Dancy

Mr. Webb—born in Shreveport, Louisiana; studied at Tulane University (M.F.A.). Ms. Dancy—born in New York City; studied at Vassar College (B.A.) and Yale University (M.F.A.). Both have designed and painted scenery for summer and winter stock and for opera productions; responsible for complete scenic production of Borodin's *Prince Igor,* Cincinnati Conservatory/New York City Opera; designed several productions in New York including 1971 revival of *Long Day's Journey into Night;* during last seven seasons they have designed eight American premieres at the Long Wharf Theatre, including *Yegor Bulichov, A Whistle in the Dark, The Contractor, Forget-Me-Not Lane, The National Health;* designed *Forget-Me-Not Lane* for Mark Taper Forum (1974); art directors for film *Cold Sweat;* Ms. Dancy has taught and designed at Vassar College and Marymount College; Mr. Webb has been a designer/consultant for NBC-TV News and Paramount Pictures television productions; they have both worked as production designers for CBS-TV.

Peter Wexler

Born in New York City; studied at Art Students League, University of Michigan School of Architecture and Design (B.S., 1958) and Yale University; has taught or lectured at the University of Michigan, State University of New York, Binghamton, and University of Arizona; has designed numerous productions in New York including *Brecht on Brecht, War and Peace, The Burnt Flower Bed, The White Devil, A Joyful Noise, The Happy Time, Minnie's Boys, The Trial of the Catonsville Nine, Murderous Angels* and *The Web and the Rock;* as principal designer and now design advisor for Center Theatre Group, Los Angeles, designed more than a dozen productions including *The Deputy, The Devils, The Marriage of Mr. Mississippi, In the Matter of J. Robert Oppenheimer, Camino Real, Godspell, Mass* and *Hamlet;* designed scenery for Far East and Eastern Europe State Department tour by Center Theatre Group; has designed scenery, lighting, interior, exterior and graphics for New York Philharmonic *Promenades* since 1965; designed spatial conception, audience design, lighting and graphics for New York Philharmonic *Rug Concerts* (1973-74); designed scenery and costumes for Lincoln Center Repertory's *Camino Real;* has designed productions for the Metropolitan Opera, New York City Opera, Washington Opera Society, Central City Opera; has designed for television and films; recent work includes scenery and lighting design for *Henry IV, Parts 1 and 2,* Goodman Theatre, and lighting for *Summer Festival '74,* Los Angeles Philharmonic at the Hollywood Bowl; currently investigating spatial and audience design concepts for Philharmonic Hall, Lincoln Center, and co-designing new Hollywood Bowl.

Ed Wittstein

Born in Mount Vernon, New York; studied at New York University (B.S.), Parsons School of Design, Cooper Union and Piscator's Dramatic Workshop, New York; Off Broadway productions include *The Fantasticks, Serjeant Musgrave's Dance, The Knack, The Last Sweet Days of Isaac, Happy Birthday, Wanda June, A Scent of Flowers* and several Pinter plays; designed *Kean, The Yearling, Enter Laughing, You Know I Can't Hear You When the Water's Running, Ulysses in Nighttown* and others on Broadway; has designed several productions for the American Shakespeare Festival including *Falstaff, As You Like It, Richard II* and *Much Ado About Nothing;* designed *The Marriage of Figaro* for New York City Opera; designed *La Bohème, Così fan tutti, Cavalleria rusticana* for NBC-TV Opera, and *A Memory of Two Mondays, A Touch of the Poet, Home* and other plays for NET-TV; production designer on several films; won Obie Award for *Serjeant Musgrave's Dance* and Tony nomination for *Ulysses in Nighttown;* has recently been concentrating on his paintings and drawings for forthcoming exhibition in New York.

Robert Yodice

Born in New York City; B.F.A., M.F.A.; studied painting with Robert Rabinowitz; assisted designers Ming Cho Lee and Wolfgang Roth (1969-70); assistant professor and resident designer, University of California (1971-72); has designed for the Joffrey Ballet, City Center Acting Company, New York Shakespeare Festival; as staff designer for the Juilliard School, designed *Ariadne auf Naxos, The Glass Menagerie,* Bloch's *Macbeth;* recent work includes set and costume designs for New York Shakespeare Festival Public Theatre production of *Where Do We Go from Here?,* and designs for Juilliard School opera productions of *Tosca* and Barber's *Antony and Cleopatra.*

Patricia Zipprodt

Born in Evanston, Illinois; studied at Wellesley College (B.A.) and Fashion Institute of Technology; has designed costumes for numerous Broadway musicals and plays including *She Loves Me, The Rope Dancers, Fiddler on the Roof, Cabaret, A Visit to a Small Planet, The Little Foxes, Scratch, Zorba, 1776* and *Pippin;* Off Broadway productions include *The Balcony, The Blacks, The Crucible* and *Oh Dad, Poor Dad;* for the Opera Company of Boston designed costumes for *La Bohème, Madama Butterfly* and others; has designed for the New York City Opera and the Guthrie Theatre; designed costumes for Jerome Robbins' ballets *Les Noces, Watermill, Dumbarton Oaks* and *Dybbuk Variations;* film work includes costume designs for *The Graduate, 1776* and *The Glass Menagerie;* recent productions designed are *Mack and Mabel* and the forthcoming *Chicago.*

PHOTO CREDITS

TEXT: "U.S. Stage Design—Past and Present": *Divine Comedy* photo courtesy Hoblitzelle Theatre Arts Library, Humanities Research Center, The University of Texas at Austin; *Macbeth, Dynamo, Oklahoma!* photos courtesy Theatre Collection, The New York Public Library at Lincoln Center, Astor, Lenox and Tilden Foundations, *Winterset* photo by Peter A. Juley & Sons; "The Designer and the Broadway Scene": *Parnell, Brigadoon, Pal Joey* photos courtesy Theatre Collection, The New York Public Library at Lincoln Center, Astor, Lenox and Tilden Foundations; "Environmental Design": *Endgame* photo by Babette Mangolte, *Makbeth* photo by Frederick Eberstadt; "Designing for Resident Theatres": *The Changing Room* photo by Van Williams, *Camino Real* photo by Walter Burton; "Notes on Designing Musicals": *Follies, A Little Night Music, Zorba, Company, Fiddler on the Roof* photos by Robert Galbraith; "Designing Opera": *Don Rodrigo* photo by Fred Fehl, *The Ballad of Baby Doe* photo by Thomas Feist, *Don Carlo, Manon Lescaut* photos courtesy *Opera News;* "Decor for Dance": *Ricercare* photo by Jack Mitchell, *Schéhérazade, Seraphic Dialogue* photos courtesy Dance Collection, The New York Public Library at Lincoln Center, Astor, Lenox and Tilden Foundations.

PLATES: *Follies* model photo by Robert Galbraith; photos by Nathan Rabin for the following: *Man of La Mancha* set design, *Henry V* costume designs, *The Hostage* model, *The Lower Depths* set and costume design, *The Visit of the Old Lady* set design, *The Karl Marx Play* set design, *Candide* set design, *The Changing Room* model, *Bartók Piano Concerto Number 3* set design, *A Little Night Music* costume designs, *Sebastian* set design, *Arco-Iris* curtain design, *The Visit* set design, *Wipe-Out Games* model, *Brain Child* model, *Dear Oscar* costume designs, *Peer Gynt* set design, *The Venetian Twins* set design, *1776* set design, *Short Eyes* model, *Neil Diamond: One Man Show* model, *Don Carlo* set design, *Die Frau ohne Schatten* set design, *The Life and Times of Joseph Stalin* set design, *The Night of the Iguana* model, *The Hot L Baltimore* set design, *The Merry Wives of Windsor* costume designs, *Makbeth* model, *Pinkville* environment design, *Macbeth* set designs, *Indians* model, *The Rise and Fall of the City of Mahagonny* set design, *Ross* costume designs, *The Beggar's Opera* set design, *The Song of the Nightingale* costume designs, *Cyrano de Bergerac* costume designs, *Rodelinda* costume designs, *The Good Doctor* costume designs, *The Iceman Cometh* model, *Les Troyens* model, *Macbeth* (opera) set design, *1776* costume design, *Waiting for Godot* costume design.

COLOR PLATES: *Follies* model photo by Robert Galbraith, *The Karl Marx Play* set design and *Julius Caesar* costume design for Lady Citizens photos by Nathan Rabin.

It is with pleasure that we acknowledge the many people and organizations who gave us expert behind-the-scenes assistance in mounting the Contemporary Stage Design–U.S.A. exhibition and in producing this book: Charles B. Froom, Betsy Lee, B. Patricia Woodbridge, Lowell Detweiller, Margery Aronson, Judith Ravel Leabo, Collins Bruce, Louis Santini and the staff of Santini Brothers Fine Arts Division, the Dance, Theatre and Music Collections of the Library and Museum of the Performing Arts at Lincoln Center, the Reference Library of the International Theatre Institute, the United Scenic Artists, Locals 829 and 350, the Scenic and Title Artists, Local 816 (IATSE), Theatre Communications Group, the Black Theatre Alliance, the Off Off Broadway Alliance and the American Association of Dance Companies.

And special thanks to all the artists who took the time to submit their work to this design project.